Workbook/Study Guide

for use with

Introduction to Managerial Accounting

Third Edition

Peter C. Brewer
Miami University

Ray H. Garrison
Brigham Young University

Eric W. Noreen
University of Washington

 **McGraw-Hill
Irwin**

Boston   Burr Ridge, IL   Dubuque, IA   Madison, WI   New York   San Francisco   St. Louis
Bangkok   Bogotá   Caracas   Kuala Lumpur   Lisbon   London   Madrid   Mexico City
Milan   Montreal   New Delhi   Santiago   Seoul   Singapore   Sydney   Taipei   Toronto

McGraw-Hill
Irwin

Workbook/Study Guide for use with
INTRODUCTION TO MANAGERIAL ACCOUNTING
Peter C. Brewer, Ray H. Garrison, and Eric W. Noreen

Published by McGraw-Hill/Irwin, an imprint of The McGraw-Hill Companies, Inc., 1221 Avenue of the Americas, New York, NY 10020. Copyright © 2007 by The McGraw-Hill Companies, Inc. All rights reserved.

1 2 3 4 5 6 7 8 9 0 BKM/BKM 0 9 8 7 6

ISBN-13: 978-0-07-326501-8
ISBN-10: 0-07-326501-2

www.mhhe.com

The McGraw-Hill Companies

Preface

To The Student

This study guide supplements the third edition of *Introduction to Managerial Accounting* by Peter C. Brewer, Eric W. Noreen, and Ray H. Garrison. Each chapter of the study guide contains three major sections:

1. The *Chapter Study Suggestions* help you study more efficiently.
2. *Chapter Highlights* summarize in outline form the essential points in a chapter.
3. *Review and Self Test* questions and exercises test your knowledge of the material in the chapter. Solutions are provided. *Caution:* If you want to score well on exams, you *must* work out each solution on your own and *then* check to see whether your solution is correct by comparing it to the solution in the study guide. You cannot learn the material by simply reading the solution provided in the study guide. This does not work.

This study guide can be used as an integral part of the process of learning the material in a chapter. When used for this purpose, we recommend that you follow the steps below:

1. Read the *Chapter Study Suggestions* in this study guide.
2. Read the textbook chapter.
3. Read the outline in the *Chapter Highlights* section of the study guide. If you run across anything in the outline you don't understand, refer back to the textbook for a more detailed discussion.
4. Work the questions and exercises in the study guide and then compare your answers to those given in the study guide. If you find something you don't understand, refer to the textbook for help.
5. Work the homework problems assigned by your instructor.

Alternatively, the study guide can also be used as a very effective way to study for exams. Before reading the chapter in your textbook, read the *Chapter Study Suggestions* in this study guide. Then lay the study guide aside until it is time to prepare for an exam. The *Chapter Highlights* section of the study guide can then be used to review the essential material covered in the chapter. The *Review and Self Test* questions and exercises are excellent practice for exams. The questions and exercises in the study guide are particularly effective used in this way since they are likely to be similar to the questions and exercises your instructor will ask on an exam.

Remember, the study guide is not a substitute for the textbook. Rather, its purpose is to *supplement* the textbook by helping you to learn the material.

Peter C. Brewer
Eric W. Noreen
Ray H. Garrison

Contents

Chapter 1

An Introduction to Managerial Accounting and Cost Concepts

Chapter Study Suggestions

This chapter discusses the work of managers and introduces cost terms that will be used throughout the book. The chapter also discusses the flow of costs in a manufacturing company. (Chapter 2 covers cost flows in more depth.) As you read the chapter, note each new term and be sure you understand its meaning. It is important to keep in mind that costs are classified in many ways, depending on how the costs will be used. This is the reason for so many different cost terms. To fit the cost terms into a framework, you should frequently refer to Exhibit 1-9 as you go through the chapter.

Exhibit 1-6 presents the *schedule of cost of goods manufactured*. You should memorize the format of this schedule, as well as the material in Exhibit 1-7. Learning this material will help you in Chapter 2 and will also lay a foundation for many chapters that follow.

CHAPTER HIGHLIGHTS

A. Managers carry out three major activities: planning, directing and motivating, and controlling.

    1. *Planning* involves identifying alternatives and selecting the best alternative.

    2. *Directing and motivating* involve mobilizing people to carry out plans and overseeing day-to-day activities.

    3. *Controlling* involves using feedback to ensure that all parts of the organization are following the plans.

B. Financial and managerial accounting differ in a number of ways. In contrast to financial accounting, managerial accounting:

    1. Focuses on providing data for internal uses.

    2. Places more emphasis on the future.

    3. Emphasizes relevance and flexibility rather than precision.

    4. Emphasizes the segments of an organization, rather than just looking at the organization as a whole.

    5. Is not governed by Generally Acceptable Accounting Practices.

    6. Is not mandatory.

C. *Manufacturing costs* are the costs of making a product and are classified as direct materials, direct labor, and manufacturing overhead.

    1. *Direct materials* are those materials that become an integral part of a finished product and can be conveniently traced into it.

        a. An example of direct materials would be the tires on a new Ford.

        b. Small material items, such as glue, are classified as *indirect materials* rather than as direct materials. It is too costly and inconvenient to trace such small costs to individual units.

    2. *Direct labor* consists of labor costs that can be easily traced to individual units of product. Direct labor is sometimes called touch labor.

        a. An example of direct labor would be a worker on a manufacturing assembly line.

        b. Other labor costs, such as supervisors and janitors, are treated as *indirect labor* rather than as direct labor. These costs cannot be traced to individual units of product since these individuals do not directly work on the product.

    3. *Manufacturing overhead* consists of all manufacturing costs except direct materials and direct labor. Manufacturing overhead includes indirect materials, indirect labor, and other manufacturing costs such as factory rent, factory utilities, and depreciation on factory equipment and facilities.

    4. The terms prime cost and conversion cost are also used to categorize manufacturing costs.

        a. *Prime cost* consists of direct materials plus direct labor.

        b. *Conversion cost* consists of direct labor plus manufacturing overhead.

D. *Nonmanufacturing costs* are those costs involved with selling and administrative activities.

    1. *Selling, or marketing, costs* include all costs associated with marketing finished products such as sales commissions, costs of delivery equipment, costs of finished goods warehouses, and advertising.

    2. *Administrative costs* include all costs associated with the general administration of an organization such as secretarial salaries, depreciation of general administrative facilities and equipment, and executive compensation.

E. For purposes of external financial reports, costs can be classified as product costs or period costs.

    1. *Period costs* are expensed on the income statement in the period in which they are incurred. (By incurred, we mean the period in which the cost is accrued, not necessarily when it is paid. For example, remember from financial accounting that salaries are counted as costs not when they are paid, but when they are earned by employees. The cost is *incurred* in the period in which it is earned. Just continue to use the rules you learned in financial accounting.)

    2. *Product costs* are matched with units of product and are recognized as an expense on the income statement only when the units are sold. Until that time, product costs are considered to be assets and are recognized on the balance sheet as inventory.

    3. In a manufacturing company, product costs include direct materials, direct labor, and manufacturing overhead. Thus, in a manufacturing company, product costs and manufacturing costs are synonymous.

    4. In a manufacturing company, period costs and nonmanufacturing costs are synonymous and selling and administrative costs are period costs.

5. In a merchandising company such as Macy's or Wal-Mart, product costs consist solely of the costs of products purchased from suppliers for resale to customers. All other costs are period costs.

F. Income statements and balance sheets prepared by manufacturing companies differ from those prepared by merchandising companies.

1. The balance sheet of a manufacturing company contains three inventory accounts: Raw Materials, Work in Process, and Finished Goods. By contrast, the balance sheet of a merchandising company contains only one inventory account—Merchandise Inventory.

a. *Raw Materials* inventory consists of materials on hand in stockrooms that will be used to make products.

b. *Work in Process* inventory consists of unfinished products.

c. *Finished Goods* inventory consists of units of product that are completed and ready for sale.

2. The income statement of a manufacturing company contains an element termed *cost of goods manufactured*. You should study the schedule of cost of goods manufactured in Exhibit 1-6 in the text very carefully.

G. Manufacturing costs (direct materials, direct labor, and overhead) are also known as *inventoriable costs* since these costs are assigned to inventories.

1. If goods are either not completed or not sold at the end of a period, these costs will be included as part of these inventory accounts on the balance sheet.

2. Study Exhibit 1-7 in the text with care. It shows the flow of manufacturing costs through inventory accounts and the way these costs become an expense (cost of goods sold) on the income statement. *This is a key exhibit for Chapter 1.*

3. We can summarize manufacturing and non-manufacturing cost terms as follows:

Synonymous Cost Terms	Costs Involved
• Manufacturing costs • Product costs • Inventoriable costs	• Direct materials, direct labor, and manufacturing overhead
• Nonmanufacturing costs • Period costs	• Selling and administrative expenses

H. Computation of cost of goods manufactured, cost of goods sold, and preparation of the income statement.

1. Computing the cost of goods sold for a manufacturing company involves a number of steps. These steps rely on the following basic model that describes flows into and out of any inventory account.

> *Basic inventory flows:*
> Beginning balance
> + Additions to inventory
> = Available
> − Ending balance
> = Withdrawals from inventory

2. To compute the raw materials used in production, this basic model is written as follows:

> Beginning balance raw materials
> + Purchases of raw materials
> = Raw materials available for use
> − Ending balance raw materials
> = Raw materials used in production

The raw materials used in production could include both direct materials and indirect materials. However, unless otherwise stated in a problem, you can assume that there are no indirect materials.

3. The next step is to compute the total manufacturing cost for the period. This is the sum of direct materials, direct labor, and manufacturing overhead costs:

> Direct materials
> + Direct labor
> + Manufacturing overhead
> = Total manufacturing cost

4. The next step is to compute the *cost of goods manufactured*. This refers to the cost of the goods that were *finished* during the period. To compute this figure, use the following version of the basic inventory flow model:

> Beginning balance, work in process
> + Total manufacturing cost
> − Ending balance, work in process
> = Cost of goods manufactured

5. The final step in the computation of cost of goods sold is also based on the inventory flow model:

> Beginning balance, finished goods
> + Cost of goods manufactured
> = Goods available for sale
> − Ending balance, finished goods
> = Cost of goods sold

6. The income statement in a manufacturing company may or may not show the computation of the cost of goods sold as above. In the summary income statement below, it is assumed that the details of the cost of goods sold computations are shown separately.

> Sales
> − Cost of goods sold
> = Gross margin
> − Selling and administrative expenses
> = Net income

I. For purposes of describing how costs behave in response to changes in activity, costs are often classified as variable or fixed. For example, one might be interested in describing how the cost of admitting patients to a hospital responds to changes in the number of patients admitted. Or, one might be interested in how much it would cost for paint in a furniture factory if the output of the factory were increased by 10%.

1. *Variable costs* vary, in total, in direct proportion to changes in the volume or level of activity within the relevant range. Exhibit 1-10 illustrates variable cost behavior. Examples of variable costs include direct materials, (usually) direct labor, commissions to salespersons, and cost of goods sold in a merchandising company such as a shoe store.

2. *Fixed costs* remain constant in total amount within the relevant range. They include, for example, depreciation, supervisory salaries, and rent. Exhibit 1-10 illustrates fixed cost behavior.

3. The *relevant range* is the range of activity within which the assumptions about cost behavior can be considered valid. If activity changes enough (for example, volume increases 1000%), even the "fixed" costs are likely to change. Such a large increase in volume would be outside the relevant range.

J. For purposes of assigning costs to objects, costs are classified as direct or indirect.

1. Managers often want to know how much something (e.g., a product, a department, or a customer) costs. The item for which a cost is desired is called a *cost object*.

2. A *direct cost* is a cost that can be easily and conveniently traced to the cost object under consideration. For example, the salaries and commissions of salespersons in a department store's shoe department would be considered direct costs of the shoe department.

3. An *indirect cost* is a cost that cannot be easily and conveniently traced to the cost object. For example, the salary of the manager of a department store would be considered an indirect cost of the shoe department and other departments.

K. For purposes of making decisions, the following cost terms are often used: differential costs, opportunity costs, and sunk costs.

1. Every decision involves choosing from among at least two alternatives. A difference in cost between two alternatives is called a *differential cost*. Only the differential costs are relevant in making a choice between two alternatives. Costs that are the same for the two alternatives are not affected by the decision and should be ignored.

2. An *opportunity cost* is the potential benefit given up by selecting one alternative over another. Opportunity costs are not recorded in accounting records. They represent a lost benefit rather than an out-of-pocket cost.

3. A *sunk cost* is a cost that has already been incurred and that cannot be changed by any decision made now or in the future. Sunk costs are never differential costs and should always be ignored when making decisions.

REVIEW AND SELF-TEST
Questions and Exercises

True or False

Enter a T or an F in the blank to indicate whether the statement is true or false.

___F___ 1. Raw materials consist of basic natural resources, such as iron ore.

___F___ 2. A supervisor's salary would be considered direct labor if the supervisor works directly in the factory

___T___ 3. Nonmanufacturing costs consist of selling costs and administrative costs.

___T___ 4. All selling and administrative costs are period costs.

___T___ 5. The terms product cost and manufacturing cost are synonymous.

___F___ 6. Cost of goods manufactured is an expense in a manufacturing company.

___T___ 7. Part of a cost such as factory depreciation may be on the balance sheet as an asset if goods are uncompleted or unsold at the end of a period.

___T___ 8. Inventoriable costs and product costs are synonymous in a manufacturing company.

___T___ 9. Total variable cost will change in proportion to changes in the level of activity.

___F___ 10. A fixed cost is constant per unit of product.

___T___ 11. Manufacturing overhead is an indirect cost with respect to units of product.

___T___ 12. Sunk costs can be either variable or fixed.

___T___ 13. Property taxes and insurance on a factory building are examples of manufacturing overhead.

Multiple Choice

Choose the best answer or response by placing the identifying letter in the space provided.

___b___ 1. If the activity level increases, one would expect the fixed cost per unit to: a) increase; b) decrease; c) remain unchanged; d) none of these.

___a___ 2. Which of the following costs would not be a period cost? a) indirect materials; b) advertising; c) administrative salaries; d) shipping costs; e) sales commissions.

___d___ 3. The term used to describe the cost of goods transferred from work in process inventory to finished goods inventory is: a) cost of goods sold; b) raw materials; c) period cost; d) cost of goods manufactured.

___c___ 4. Manufacturing cost is synonymous with all of the following terms except: a) product cost; b) inventoriable cost; c) period cost; d) all of the above are synonymous terms.

___b___ 5. If the activity level drops by 5%, one would expect the variable costs: a) to increase per unit of product; b) to drop in total by 5%; c) to remain constant in total; d) to decrease per unit of product.

___b___ 6. All of the following are considered to be product costs for financial reporting except: a) indirect materials; b) advertising; c) rent on factory space; d) idle time; e) all of the above would be product costs.

___b___ 7. Walston Manufacturing Company has provided the following data concerning its raw materials inventories last month:

Beginning raw materials inventory..........	$80,000
Purchases of raw materials......................	$420,000
Ending raw materials inventory...............	$50,000

The cost of the raw materials used in production for the month was: a) $500,000; b) $450,000; c) $390,000; d) $470,000.

___d___ 8. Juniper Company has provided the following data concerning its manufacturing costs and work in process inventories last month:

Raw materials used in production	$270,000
Direct labor..	$140,000
Manufacturing overhead............................	$190,000
Beginning work in process inventory........	$50,000
Ending work in process inventory.............	$80,000

The cost of goods manufactured for the month was: a) $730,000; b) $630,000; c) $600,000; d) $570,000.

___a___ 9. Vonder Inc. has provided the following data concerning its finished goods inventories last month:

Beginning finished goods inventory..........	$110,000
Cost of goods manufactured......................	$760,000
Ending finished goods inventory...............	$70,000

The cost of goods sold for the month was: a) $800,000; b) $720,000; c) $950,000; d) $280,000.

Exercises

1-1.   Classify each of the following costs as either period costs or product costs. Also indicate whether the cost is fixed or variable with respect to changes in the amount of output produced and sold.

		Period Cost	Product Cost	Variable Cost	Fixed Cost
-	Example: Rent on a sales office	X			X
-	Example: Direct materials		X	X	
a.	Sales commissions	X		X	
b.	Rent on a factory building		X		X
c.	Headquarters secretarial salaries	X			X
d.	Assembly line workers		X	X	
e.	Product advertising	X		X	X
f.	Cherries in a cannery		X	X	
g.	Top management salaries	X			X
h.	Lubricants for machines		X	X	
i.	Shipping costs via express service	X		X	
j.	Executive training program	X	X	X	X
k.	Factory supervisory salaries	X	X		X

1-2.   Using the following data and the form that appears below, prepare a schedule of cost of goods manufactured.

Lubricants for machines	$4,500
Rent, factory building	$16,000
Direct labor	$90,000
Indirect materials	$2,000
Sales commissions	$24,600
Factory utilities	$5,800
Insurance, factory	$2,000
Purchases of raw materials	$120,000
Work in process, beginning	$16,000
Work in process, ending	$11,500
Raw materials, beginning	$15,000
Raw materials, ending	$5,000
Depreciation of office equipment	$4,000

Schedule of Cost of Goods Manufactured

(See Exhibit 1-6 in the text for the proper format)

Direct materials:

Raw Mat Begi .... $ 15,000

+ Raw Mat pur. 120000

.... 135000

− end raw Mat 5000

.... 130000

Direct labor................................ 90,000

Manufacturing overhead:

Lubricants for Machines 4500

.... 16,000

.... 2000

.... 5800

.... 2000

.... 30,300

250300

+ Begi work in process 16,000

266300

− End work in process 11500

Cost of Goods Manufactured........................ $ 254800

1-3.   Harry is considering whether to produce and sell classic wooden surfboards in his spare time. He has a garage that was constructed at a cost of $12,000 several years ago, and which could be used for production purposes. The garage would be depreciated over a 20-year life. Harry has determined that each surfboard will require $30 in wood. He would hire students to do most of the work and pay them $35 for each surfboard completed. He would rent tools at a cost of $400 per month. Harry can draw money out of savings to provide the capital needed to get the operation going. The savings are earning interest at 6% annually. An ad agency would handle advertising at a cost of $500 per month. Harry would hire students to sell the surfboards and pay a commission of $20 per board.

Required:

From the foregoing information, identify all the examples you can of the following types of costs (a single item may be identified as many types of costs). A cost should be classified as variable in this case if it is variable with respect to the number of surfboards produced and sold. A cost should be classified as a differential cost if it differs between the alternatives of producing or not producing the surfboards.

	Variable cost	Fixed cost	Selling & admin. cost	Product cost	Manuf. ovhd. cost	Sunk cost	Opportunity cost	Differential cost
Original cost of garage	___	___	___	___	___	___	___	___
Depreciation on the garage	___	___	___	___	___	___	___	___
Wood for each surfboard	___	___	___	___	___	___	___	___
Student workers	___	___	___	___	___	___	___	___
Tool rental	___	___	___	___	___	___	___	___
Interest on savings	___	___	___	___	___	___	___	___
Advertising costs	___	___	___	___	___	___	___	___
Sales commissions	___	___	___	___	___	___	___	___

Answers to Questions and Exercises

True or False

1. F   Raw materials consist of any materials used to make a product. The finished goods of one company can be the raw materials of another company.

2. F   Direct labor can be physically traced to products in a "hands on" sense. Supervisors do not work directly on products and therefore are not direct labor.

3. T   Nonmanufacturing cost is synonymous with selling and administrative costs.

4. T   Selling and administrative costs are period costs because they are charged against income in the period in which they are incurred rather than being added to the cost of manufactured or purchased goods.

5. T   These two terms are synonymous.

6. F   Cost of goods manufactured is not an expense. It is the amount transferred from work in process to finished goods inventory when goods are completed. This is a subtle, but important, point.

7. T   Manufacturing costs are assigned to units during production. If these units are not complete or not sold at the end of a period, then the manufacturing costs incurred to date are included as part of Work in Process or Finished Goods inventories which are assets on the balance sheet.

8. T   These two terms are synonymous.

9. T   Since a variable cost is constant per unit, it will change in total in proportion to changes in the level of activity. If activity increases by 5%, then the total variable cost should also increase by 5%.

10. F   A fixed cost is constant in total amount; on a per unit basis, it varies inversely with changes in the level of activity.

11. T   Manufacturing overhead cost is an indirect cost; only direct materials and direct labor are direct manufacturing costs.

12. T   A sunk cost is a cost that has already been incurred and can be variable or fixed. If obsolete materials have already been purchased, for example, then the cost of the materials is a sunk cost.

13. T   Manufacturing overhead consists of all production costs except direct materials and direct labor.

Multiple Choice

1. b   The fixed cost per unit should drop since a constant amount is spread over more units.

2. a   Indirect materials are part of manufacturing overhead and thus are included in product costs.

3. d   The cost of goods manufactured refers to the costs of goods that are completed and ready for sale during the period.

4. c   A period cost represents a cost charged against the period in which the cost is incurred; it has nothing to do with the manufacture of a product.

5. b   By definition, total variable cost changes in proportion to changes in activity.

6. b   Advertising is a period cost, rather than a product cost.

7. b   The computations are as follows:

Beginning raw materials inventory	$ 80,000
Add: Purchases of raw materials	420,000
Raw materials available for use	500,000
Deduct: Ending raw materials inventory	50,000
Raw materials used in production	$450,000

8. d   The computations are as follows:

Raw materials used in production	$270,000
Direct labor	140,000
Manufacturing overhead	190,000
Total manufacturing costs	600,000
Add: Beginning work in process inventory	50,000
	650,000
Deduct: Ending work in process inventory	80,000
Cost of goods manufactured	$570,000

9. a   The cost of goods sold is computed as follows:

Beginning finished goods inventory	$110,000
Add: Cost of goods manufactured	760,000
Goods available for sale	870,000
Deduct: Ending finished goods inventory	70,000
Cost of goods sold	$800,000

Exercises

1-1.

		Period Cost	Product Cost	Variable Cost	Fixed Cost
a.	Sales commissions	X		X	
b.	Rent on a factory building		X		X
c.	Headquarters secretarial salaries	X			X
d.	Assembly line workers		X	X	
e.	Product advertising	X			X
f.	Cherries in a cannery		X	X	
g.	Top management salaries	X			X
h.	Lubricants for machines		X	X	
i.	Shipping costs via express service	X		X	
j.	Executive training program	X			X
k.	Factory supervisory salaries		X		X

1-2. Direct materials:

Raw materials inventory, beginning	$ 15,000	
Add: Purchases of raw materials	120,000	
Raw materials available for use	135,000	
Deduct: Raw materials inventory, ending	5,000	
Raw materials used in production		$130,000
Direct labor		90,000
Manufacturing overhead:		
Lubricants for machines	4,500	
Rent, factory building	16,000	
Indirect materials	2,000	
Factory utilities	5,800	
Insurance, factory	2,000	
Total manufacturing overhead costs		30,300
Total manufacturing costs		250,300
Add: Work in process, beginning		16,000
		266,300
Deduct: Work in process, ending		11,500
Cost of Goods Manufactured		$254,800

Note: Sales commissions and depreciation on office equipment are not manufacturing costs.

1-3.

	Variable cost	Fixed cost	Selling & admin. cost	Product cost	Manuf. ovhd. cost	Sunk cost	Opportunity cost	Differential cost
Original cost of garage						X		
Depreciation on the garage		X		X	X			(1)
Wood for each surfboard	X			X				X
Student workers	X			X				X
Tool rental		X		X	X			X
Interest on savings							X	(2)
Advertising costs		X	X					X
Sales commissions	X		X					X

(1) This is not a differential cost if the depreciation on the garage is the same regardless of whether it is used to make surfboards or is used conventionally as a residential garage.

(2) This may be considered to be a differential cost, although some would say that it is not since it is a foregone benefit rather than a cost *per se*.

Chapter 2

Systems Design: Job-Order Costing

Chapter Study Suggestions

This chapter expands on the concepts introduced in Chapter 1 and provides more details concerning how product costs are determined. The costing method illustrated in the chapter is known as *job-order costing*. Exhibit 2-5 provides a overall view of the flow of cost and the documents in a job-order cost system. Pay particular attention to the section in the chapter titled "Application of Manufacturing Overhead." *Overhead application is a key concept in the chapter.*

Exhibits 2-6, 2-7, and 2-8 show how direct materials, direct labor, and overhead costs are assigned to jobs. Study these exhibits with particular care—the concepts they contain will show up often in the homework material. Exhibits 2-10 and 2-11 summarize these concepts. Note particularly the difference between the schedule of cost of goods manufactured in Exhibit 2-11 and the schedule of cost of goods manufactured in Chapter 1. Study and then *restudy* the section titled "Underapplied and Overapplied Overhead," paying particular attention to how underapplied and overapplied overhead is computed.

CHAPTER HIGHLIGHTS

A. Two basic costing systems are commonly used in manufacturing and in many service organizations: process costing and job-order costing.

   1. *Process costing* is used in situations where a single homogeneous product such as bricks is produced for long periods of time.

   2. *Job-order costing* is used in situations where many different products or services are produced each period. Examples include special order printing and custom furniture manufacturing. For example, fifty units of a particular type of sofa might be made in one batch. Each batch is called a "job." These concepts also extend to service companies. For example, in a consulting company, a job would be a particular consulting project.

B. We will begin our discussion of job-order costing with raw materials. When materials are purchased, their costs are recorded in the Raw Materials inventory account, which is an asset.

   1. Materials are withdrawn from storage using a *materials requisition form* as authorization. This form lists all the materials required to complete a specific job. The journal entry to record withdrawal of raw materials from the storeroom for use in production is:

Work in Process (direct materials)	XXX	
Manuf. Ovhd. (indirect materials)	XXX	
Raw Materials		XXX

Materials that are traced directly to jobs are classified as *direct materials* and are debited to Work in Process. Any materials that are not directly traced to jobs are classified as *indirect materials* and are debited to a special control account called *Manufacturing Overhead.*

   2. When materials are placed into production, they are recorded on a *job cost sheet*, which summarizes all production costs assigned to a particular job. Exhibit 2-2 in the text illustrates a job cost sheet.

C. Labor costs are recorded on *time tickets* or *time sheets* that are filled out by employees. These documents list the amount of time each employee works on specific jobs and tasks.

   1. Labor time spent working directly on specific jobs is termed *direct labor*. Labor time spent working on supportive tasks (e.g., supervision, maintenance, janitorial) is termed *indirect labor*. The entry to record labor costs is:

Work in Process (direct labor)	XXX	
Manuf. Ovhd. (indirect labor)	XXX	
Salaries and Wages Payable		XXX

   2. Direct labor costs are added to the individual job cost sheets at the same time they are recorded in the formal accounts.

D. As explained in Chapter 1, manufacturing overhead is an *indirect* cost and therefore must be allocated in order to be assigned to units of product. This allocation is usually done with a *predetermined overhead rate.*

   1. The predetermined overhead rate is computed *before* the year begins and is based entirely on estimated data. Ordinarily, the rate is computed for an entire year to eliminate seasonal fluctuations. The formula is:

$$\text{Predetermined overhead rate} = \frac{\text{Estimated total manufacturing overhead cost}}{\text{Estimated total amount of the allocation base}}$$

An *allocation base* is a measure of activity, such as direct labor-hours, direct labor cost, or machine-hours. The allocation base is something that all jobs have in common—for example, all of the jobs may require direct labor-hours. Ideally, the allocation base should actually cause the overhead cost, but in practice this ideal is often ignored.

   2. Suppose direct labor-hours is the allocation base and that the estimated total manufacturing overhead cost for next year is $400,000 and the estimated total number of direct labor-hours is 10,000. Then the predetermined overhead rate would be $40 per direct labor-hour ($400,000 ÷ 10,000 direct labor-hours).

   3. To assign overhead costs to a job, the predetermined overhead rate is multiplied by the amount of the allocation base incurred by the job. For example, suppose that a particular job incurs 20 direct labor-hours and the predetermined overhead rate is $40 per direct labor-hour. Then $800 (20 direct labor-hours × $40 per direct labor-hour) of overhead cost would be *applied* to that job. This $800 is called the *overhead applied*. Note that this is not actual overhead spending on the job. The $800 may have little to do with any overhead that is actually caused by the job. It is simply a way of distributing the overhead costs that were estimated at the beginning of the year among the jobs worked on during the year.

   4. The overhead that is applied to a job is entered on its job cost sheet and is recorded in the company's formal accounts with the following journal entry:

Work in Process	XXX	
Manufacturing Overhead		XXX

5. Turn to Exhibit 2-8 in the text to see how overhead costs flow through the accounts and onto the job cost sheets. Notice from the exhibit that applying overhead to jobs and recording actual overhead costs represent two separate and distinct processes. *This is a key concept!*

6. Actual overhead costs are *not* charged to Work in Process. Instead, they are charged to the Manufacturing Overhead control account as we saw in the entries for indirect labor and indirect materials above. Note that *actual overhead costs all appear as debits to Manufacturing Overhead.*

E. When jobs are completed, their costs are transferred from Work in Process to Finished Goods. The journal entry is:

Finished Goods	XXX	
Work in Process		XXX

When completed products are sold, their costs are transferred from Finished Goods to Cost of Goods Sold. The journal entry is:

Cost of Goods Sold	XXX	
Finished Goods		XXX

F. Exhibits 2-10, 2-11 and 2-12 are key exhibits that summarize much of the material in the chapter. Study these exhibits with care. Note particularly how the manufacturing overhead costs are handled.

G. Generally the amount of overhead cost *applied* to Work in Process differs from the amount of *actual* overhead cost. This difference will be reflected in a debit or credit balance in the Manufacturing Overhead account.

1. If less overhead cost is applied to Work in Process than has actually been incurred, then overhead has been *underapplied* and the Manufacturing Overhead account has a debit balance.

2. If more overhead cost is applied to Work in Process than has actually been incurred, then overhead has been *overapplied* and the Manufacturing Overhead account has a credit balance.

3. Underapplied or overapplied overhead can be computed as follows:

Actual overhead costs	$XXX
Less: Overhead costs applied to Work in Process*	XXX
Underapplied (overapplied) overhead..........	$XXX

* Predetermined overhead rate × Actual amount of the allocation base incurred during the period.

4. At the end of a period, underapplied or overapplied overhead is closed out to Cost of Goods Sold

a. If overhead has been underapplied, the entry would be:

Cost of Goods Sold	XXX	
Manufacturing Overhead		XXX

This entry increases Cost of Goods Sold. If overhead has been underapplied, not enough overhead cost was applied to jobs during the period and therefore costs are understated in the accounts. The journal entry above adjusts Cost of Goods Sold so that it is no longer understated.

b. If overhead has been overapplied, the journal entry would be:

Manufacturing Overhead	XXX	
Cost of Goods Sold		XXX

This entry decreases Cost of Goods Sold. If overhead has been overapplied, too much overhead cost was applied to jobs during the period and therefore costs are overstated in the accounts. The journal entry above adjusts Cost of Goods Sold so that it is no longer overstated.

H. Largely for simplicity, the chapter assumes that a single "plant-wide" overhead rate is used. Many companies use *multiple overhead rates* rather than a single plant wide rate. Each production department or work center may have its own predetermined overhead rate and its own allocation base. These more complex systems will be investigated in the chapter dealing with activity-based costing.

REVIEW AND SELF-TEST
Questions and Exercises

True or False

Enter a T or an F in the blank to indicate whether the statement is true or false.

__T__ 1. A company producing many different kinds of furniture would probably use a job-order cost system.

__T__ 2. Process costing systems are used in situations where output is homogeneous—the company makes a single product for long periods of time.

__F__ 3. Most factory overhead costs are direct costs that can be easily identified with specific jobs.

__T__ 4. The predetermined overhead rate is computed using estimates of overhead cost and the amount of the allocation base.

__F__ 5. The predetermined overhead rate is generally computed on a monthly basis rather than on an annual basis to increase the accuracy of unit costs.

__T__ 6. The cost of indirect materials used in production is added to the Manufacturing Overhead account rather than to Work in Process.

__T__ 7. The job cost sheet is used to accumulate the costs charged to a particular job.

__F__ 8. Actual manufacturing overhead costs are charged directly to the Work in Process account as the costs are incurred.

__F__ 9. Selling and administrative expenses are charged to the Manufacturing Overhead account.

__T__ 10. If more manufacturing overhead is applied to Work in Process than is actually incurred, then overhead cost will be overapplied.

__T__ 11. A debit balance in the Manufacturing Overhead account at the end of a period would mean that overhead was underapplied for the period.

__T__ 12. Underapplied or overapplied overhead is computed by finding the difference between actual overhead costs and the amount of overhead cost applied to Work in Process.

Multiple Choice

Choose the best answer or response by placing the identifying letter in the space provided.

__b__ 1. In a job-order costing system, the basic document for accumulating costs for a specific job is: a) the materials requisition form; b) the job cost sheet; c) the Work in Process inventory account; d) the labor time ticket.

__b__ 2. Suppose $30,000 of raw materials are purchased. What account is debited? a) Work in Process inventory; b) Raw Materials inventory; c) Cost of Goods Sold; d) Manufacturing Overhead.

__d__ 3. Suppose $20,000 of raw materials are withdrawn from the storeroom to be used in production. Of this amount, $15,000 consists of direct materials and $5,000 consists of indirect materials. What account or accounts will be debited? a) Work in Process $15,000 and Raw Materials $5,000; b) Raw Materials $15,000 and Manufacturing Overhead $5,000; c) Manufacturing Overhead $15,000 and Work in Process $5,000; d) Work in Process $15,000 and Manufacturing Overhead $5,000.

__a__ 4. Suppose $70,000 of wages and salaries are earned by employees. Of this amount, $20,000 consists of direct labor; $10,000 consists of indirect labor; and $40,000 consists of administrative salaries. What account or accounts will be debited? a) Work in Process $20,000 and Manufacturing Overhead $10,000 and Administrative Salary Expense $40,000; b) Direct Labor $20,000 and Indirect Labor $10,000 and Administrative Salary Expense $40,000; c) Work in Process $20,000 and Manufacturing Overhead $50,000; d) Direct Labor $20,000 and Manufacturing Overhead $50,000.

__d__ 5. Suppose jobs are completed whose job cost sheets total $120,000. What account will be debited? a) Manufacturing Overhead $120,000; b) Cost of Goods Sold $120,000; c) Work in Process $120,000; d) Finished Goods $120,000.

__c__ 6. Suppose a total of $30,000 of overhead is applied to jobs. What account will be debited? a) Manufacturing Overhead $30,000; b) Cost of Goods Sold $30,000; c) Work in Process $30,000; d) Finished Goods $30,000.

_C_ 7. Last year, a company reported estimated overhead, $100,000; actual overhead, $90,000; and applied overhead, $92,000. The company's overhead cost for the year would be: a) underapplied, $10,000; b) underapplied, $8,000; c) overapplied, $2,000; d) overapplied, $10,000.

_a_ 8. Jurden Company bases its predetermined overhead rate on machine hours. At the beginning of the year, the company estimated its manufacturing overhead for the year would be $60,000 and its machine hours would be 40,000. Actual manufacturing overhead for year amounted to $65,100 and the actual machine hours totaled 42,000. Manufacturing overhead for the year would be: a) underapplied by $2,100; b) overapplied by $3,000; c) underapplied by $3,000; d) overapplied by $5,100.

_____ 9. On January 1, Hessler Company's Work in Process account had a balance of $18,000. During the year, direct materials costing $35,000 were placed into production. Direct labor cost for the year was $60,000.

The predetermined overhead rate for the year was set at 150% of direct labor cost. Actual overhead costs for the year totaled $92,000. Jobs costing $190,000 to manufacture according to their job cost sheets were completed during the year. On December 31, the balance in the Work in Process inventory account would be: a) $13,000; b) $18,000; c) $15,000; d) $8,000.

_b_ 10. The Cost of Goods Manufactured represents: a) the amount of cost charged to Work in Process during the period; b) the amount transferred from Work in Process to Finished Goods during the period; c) the amount of cost placed into production during the period; d) none of these.

_C_ 11. If overhead is overapplied for a period, it means that: a) the predetermined overhead rate used to apply overhead cost to Work in Process was too low; b) the company incurred more overhead cost than it charged to Work in Process; c) too much cost has been assigned to jobs; d) none of these.

Exercises

2-1. Bartle Company uses a job-order cost system and applies overhead with a predetermined overhead rate based on direct labor-hours. At the beginning of the year the estimated total manufacturing overhead for the year was $150,000 and the estimated level of activity was 100,000 direct labor-hours. At the end of the year, cost records revealed that actual overhead costs of $160,000 had been incurred and that 105,000 direct labor hours had been worked.

a. The predetermined overhead rate for the year was $_____1.5_____

b. Manufacturing overhead cost applied to work in process during the year was$_____157500_____

c. The amount of underapplied or overapplied overhead cost for the year was $_____2500_____

2-2. The following selected account balances are taken from the books of Pardoe Company as of January 1 of the most recent year:

Cash

12,000	760000
790000	
802000	802000
Bal 42000	

Work in Process

40,000	550000
145000	
250000	
165000	
600000	600000
Bal 50000	

Accounts Payable

300000	75,000
	150000
	50,000
	35000
	30000
	25000
810000	810000
	510000

Sales

	800000
800000	800000

Accounts Receivable

48,000	790000
800000	
848000	848000
Bal 58000	

Finished Goods

100,000	540000
550000	
650000	650000
Bal 110000	

Salaries and Wages Payable

460000	12,000
	465000
477000	477000

Cost of Goods Sold

540000	6,000

Prepaid Insurance

8,000	4000
8000	8000
4000	

Accumulated Depreciation

	120,000
	20,000
140000	140000

Advertis

50,000	
50,000	50,000

Selling & admi

140000	
5000	
85000	
460000	
630000	630000

Raw Materials

30,000	145000
150000	
180000	180000
Bal 35000	

Manufacturing Overhead

35000	165000
75000	
15000	
30000	
4000	
165000	
165000	165000
6,000	Bal 6,000

The following data relate to the activities of Pardoe Company during the year:
1. Raw materials purchased on account, $150,000.
2. Raw materials issued to production, $145,000 (all direct materials).
3. Advertising cost incurred for the year, $50,000 (credit accounts payable).
4. Utilities cost incurred for the factory, $35,000 (credit accounts payable).
5. Salaries and wages costs incurred: direct labor, $250,000 (30,000 hours); indirect labor, $75,000; selling and administrative, $140,000.
6. Depreciation recorded for the year, $20,000, of which 75% related to the factory and 25% related to selling and administrative functions.
7. Other factory overhead costs incurred for the year, $30,000 (credit accounts payable).
8. Other selling and administrative expenses incurred for the year, $25,000 (credit accounts payable).
9. Prepaid insurance of $4,000 expired during the year; all of this is related to the factory.
10. The company applies overhead on the basis of direct labor-hours at $5.50 per hour.
11. The cost of goods manufactured for the year totaled $550,000.
12. Goods that cost $540,000 according to their job cost sheets were sold on account for $800,000.
13. Collections on account from customers during the year totaled $790,000.
14. Cash disbursed during the year: on accounts payable, $300,000; for salaries and wages, $460,000.

Required:
a. Post the above entries directly to Pardoe Company's T-accounts on the previous page. Key your entries with the numbers 1-14.
b. Compute the ending balance in each T-account.
c. Is overhead underapplied or overapplied for the year? Close the balance to Cost of Goods Sold. (Key the entry as #15.)
d. Prepare an income statement for the year using the form that appears below.

Pardoe Company
Income Statement

Sales	$800,000
Cost of goods sold	534000
Gross margin	266000

Selling and administrative expenses:

_____ 50000	$_____	
_____ 140000	_____	
_____ 5000	_____	
_____ 25,000	_____	220000
Net operating income		$ 46,000

2-3. The following data were taken from the Precision Milling Machine, Inc., cost records for the current year. Compute the amount of raw materials used in production during the year:

Raw materials inventory, beginning.........................	$10,000
Raw materials inventory, ending...........................	$15,000
Purchases of raw materials.....................................	$145,000

$$10,000$$
$$+\ 145000$$
$$155000$$
$$-\ 15,000$$
$$140,000 \quad \text{Raw Material}$$

2-4. Suppose all of the raw materials used in production by Precision Milling Machine in the preceding exercise were direct materials. The company has supplied the following additional information:

Direct labor cost...	$240,000
Manufacturing overhead applied..............................	$90,000
Work in process inventory, beginning	$60,000
Work in process inventory, ending...........................	$75,000

Compute the cost of goods manufactured for the year.

Direct Mat.   140000
Direct Labour   240000
Man. O.H.   90,000
                     470000
+ work in process beg)   60,000
                     530000
− Work in process End,   75000
    Good Manu   455000

2-5.   Precision Milling Machine company has supplied the following additional information. Use this data together with your answer to exercise 2-4 above to compute the (adjusted) Cost of Goods Sold for the company. Close out any balance in Manufacturing Overhead to Cost of Goods Sold.

Actual manufacturing overhead incurred	$88,000
Finished goods inventory, beginning	$120,000
Finished goods inventory, ending	$145,000

Finished good Inv   120000
+ Cost of good Manu.   455000
                                     575000
- Finished good Inv end   145000
Unadjusted Cost of good sold   430000
- M.O.H. Overapplied   2000
adjusted Cost of good sold   428000

Answers to Questions and Exercises

True or False

1. **T** Job-order costing is used when many different kinds of products are made.

2. **T** Process costing is generally used when output is homogeneous.

3. **F** Only direct materials and direct labor are direct costs; manufacturing overhead cannot be easily identified with specific jobs.

4. **T** Estimates are used since a rate must be developed before the period begins.

5. **F** The predetermined overhead rate is usually computed on an annual basis to smooth out month-to-month variations in cost and activity.

6. **T** Indirect costs are charged to the Manufacturing Overhead account.

7. **T** A separate job cost sheet is prepared for each job entered into production, and is used to accumulate costs as they are charged to the job.

8. **F** Actual manufacturing overhead costs are charged to the Manufacturing Overhead account—not to Work in Process.

9. **F** Selling and administrative expenses are period costs, not product costs; thus, they are deducted as expenses on the income statement in the period they are incurred.

10. **T** This is true by definition.

11. **T** A debit balance in Manufacturing Overhead would mean that more overhead cost was incurred than was applied to Work in Process. Thus, manufacturing overhead would be underapplied.

12. **T** By definition, this is how underapplied or overapplied overhead cost is computed.

Multiple Choice

1. **b** The job cost sheet is used to accumulate direct materials, direct labor, and overhead costs.

2. **b** The journal entry would be:

Raw Materials	30,000	
Cash or Accounts Payable		30,000

3. **d** The journal entry would be:

Work in Process	15,000	
Manufacturing Overhead	5,000	
Raw Materials		20,000

4. **a** The journal entry would be:

Work in Process	20,000	
Manufacturing Overhead	10,000	
Administrative Salaries Expense	40,000	
Wages and Salaries Payable		70,000

5. **d** The journal entry would be:

Finished Goods	120,000	
Work in Process		120,000

6. **c** The journal entry would be:

Work in Process	30,000	
Manufacturing Overhead		30,000

7. **c** Underapplied or overapplied overhead represents the difference between actual overhead cost and applied overhead cost. The computation in this case would be:

Actual overhead cost	$90,000
Applied overhead cost	92,000
Overapplied overhead cost	$(2,000)

8. a The predetermined overhead rate is $60,000 ÷ 40,000 hours = $1.50 per hour.

Actual overhead cost	$65,100
Applied overhead cost ($1.50 × 42,000 hours)	63,000
Underapplied overhead cost	$ 2,100

9. a The solution would be:

Work in Process			
Balance	18,000	Finished	190,000
Direct materials	35,000		
Direct labor	60,000		
Overhead applied*	90,000		
Balance	13,000		

*$60,000 × 150% = $90,000

10. b The cost of goods manufactured represents the costs of goods completed during a period; thus, it is the amount transferred from Work in Process to Finished Goods.

11. c If overhead is overapplied, then more overhead cost has been added to jobs than has been incurred. Therefore, too much overhead cost will have been assigned to jobs.

Exercises

2-1. a. $\dfrac{\$150,000}{100,000 \text{ DLHs}} = \$1.50 \text{ per DLH}$

b. 105,000 DLHS × $1.50 per DLH = $157,500 applied

c.
Actual overhead cost	$160,000
Applied overhead cost	157,500
Underapplied overhead cost	$ 2,500

2-2. The answers to parts (a) and (b) are on the following page.

c. Overhead is overapplied by $6,000.

d.

Pardoe Company
Income Statement

Sales		$800,000
Cost of goods sold ($540,000 − $6,000)		534,000
Gross margin		266,000
Selling and administrative expenses:		
Advertising expense	$ 50,000	
Salaries expense	140,000	
Depreciation expense	5,000	
Other expenses	25,000	220,000
Net operating income		$ 46,000

2-3.
Raw materials inventory, beginning	$ 10,000
Add: Purchases of raw materials	145,000
Total	155,000
Deduct: Raw materials inventory, ending	15,000
Raw materials used in production	$140,000

2-2.   a. & b.

	Cash		
Bal.	12,000	(14)	760,000
(13)	790,000		
	42,000		

	Accumulated Depreciation		
		Bal.	120,000
		(6)	20,000
			140,000

	Sales		
		(12a)	800,000

	Accounts Receivable		
Bal.	48,000	(13)	790,000
(12a)	800,000		
	58,000		

	Manufacturing Overhead		
(4)	35,000	(10)	165,000
(5)	75,000		
(6)	15,000		
(7)	30,000		
(9)	4,000		
(15	6,000		6,000

	Cost of Goods Sold		
(12b)	540,000	(15)	6,000
	534,000		

	Prepaid insurance		
Bal.	8,000	(9)	4,000
	4,000		

	Salaries Expense		
(5)	140,000		

	Raw Materials		
Bal.	30,000	(2)	145,000
(1)	150,000		
	35,000		

	Accounts Payable		
(14)	300,000	Bal.	75,000
		(1)	150,000
		(3)	50,000
		(4)	35,000
		(7)	30,000
		(8)	25,000
			65,000

	Advertising Expense		
(3)	50,000		

	Work in Process		
Bal.	40,000	(11)	550,000
(2)	145,000		
(5)	250,000		
(10)	165,000		
	50,000		

	Depreciation Expense		
(6)	5,000		

	Finished Goods		
Bal.	100,000	(12b)	540,000
(11)	550,000		
	110,000		

	Salaries and Wages Payable		
(14)	460,000	Bal.	12,000
		(5)	465,000
			17,000

	Other Selling and Administrative Expenses		
(8)	25,000		

2-4.

Direct materials	$140,000
Direct labor	240,000
Manufacturing overhead applied	90,000
Total manufacturing cost	470,000
Add: Beginning work in process inventory	60,000
	530,000
Deduct: Ending work in process inventory	75,000
Cost of goods manufactured	$455,000

2-5.

Finished goods inventory, beginning	$120,000
Add: Cost of goods manufactured	455,000
Goods available for sale	575,000
Deduct: Finished goods, ending	145,000
Unadjusted cost of goods sold	430,000
Deduct: Overapplied overhead (see below)	2,000
Adjusted cost of goods sold	$428,000

Actual manufacturing overhead cost incurred	$88,000
Applied manufacturing overhead cost	90,000
Overapplied overhead cost	($ 2,000)

Chapter 3

Systems Design: Activity-Based Costing

Chapter Study Suggestions

Activity-based costing is an extension of the product costing methods described in Chapter 2 where overhead was assigned to products using a single predetermined overhead rate. In activity-based costing, more than one predetermined overhead rate is used to assign manufacturing overhead costs to products. Each predetermined overhead rate has its own allocation base.

CHAPTER HIGHLIGHTS

A. Overhead costs can be applied to products using a plantwide overhead rate, departmental overhead rates, or activity-based costing.

1. A *plantwide overhead rate* includes all the manufacturing overhead costs in a factory and is typically based on direct labor-hours or machine-hours. This is the method covered in Chapter 2. A plantwide overhead rate results in distorted product costs when overhead costs aren't really caused by the allocation base—be it direct labor-hours or machine-hours.

2. *Departmental overhead rates* provide a slightly more sophisticated approach than the plantwide overhead rate. Rather than a single predetermined overhead rate for the entire factory, each department has its own predetermined overhead rate. However, the allocation bases are usually still either direct labor-hours or machine-hours. So cost distortion occurs if overhead costs are caused by factors other than direct labor-hours or machine-hours. Activity-based costing attempts to correct distortions in product costs by allocating costs based on the activities that give rise to costs.

3. In *activity-based costing*, each major activity that causes overhead costs has its own activity cost pool, with its own allocation base and its own predetermined overhead rate.

   a.   An *activity* is any event or transaction that causes the incurrence of overhead cost. For example, the activity of setting up a machine causes setup costs. The key concept in activity-based costing is that products cause activities that in turn consume resources and the consumption of these resources causes costs.

   b.   An *activity cost pool* in activity-based costing is an overhead pool containing all of the costs associated with a particular activity.

   c.   Activity-based costing involves two stages of allocation. In the first stage of the allocation process, costs are assigned to the activity cost pools. This part of the allocation process is not covered in the text.

   c.   In the second stage of the allocation process, the costs in each activity cost pool are assigned to products according to the amount of activity each product requires. This is accomplished by computing an *activity rate* (i.e., predetermined overhead rate) for each activity cost pool. For example, the total cost in the machine setup cost pool might be $150,000 and the total activity might be 1,000 setups. In that case, the activity rate would be $150 per setup and if a product requires two setups, it would be charged $300 for setups.

B. To understand the implications of activity-based costing, it is helpful to categorize activities into a hierarchy consisting of unit-level, batch-level, product-level, and facility-level activities.

   a.   *Unit-level activities* are performed each time a unit is produced. For example, shaping a part for a product on a milling machine would be a unit-level activity.

   b.   *Batch-level activities* are performed each time a batch is handled or processed. For example, purging black paint from a spray-painting machine prior to running a batch of red auto panels is a batch-level activity. Costs in a batch-level cost pool depend on the number of batches run, but not on the number of units in a batch.

   c.   *Product-level activities* are required to have a product at all. An example would be maintaining an up-to-date parts list and instruction manual for the product. Costs in a product-level cost pool depend on the number of products or their complexity, but not the number of batches run or the number of units.

   d.   *Facility-level activities* sustain a facility's general manufacturing processes. For example, maintaining the factory grounds is a facility-level activity.

C. Traditional allocation bases such as direct labor-hours tend to allocate overhead costs to the highest volume products simply because they are responsible for the largest number of direct labor-hours. However, if overhead costs are actually caused by batch-level or product-level activities, allocating costs to the highest volume products will seriously distort product costs.

   a.   For example, batch-level costs are incurred irrespective of how many units are in a batch. Consequently, a batch with many units should be charged the same amount as a batch with only one unit. However, allocating batch-level costs on the basis of direct labor-hours or machine-hours will generally result in inappropriately allocating more batch-level costs to large batches than small batches.

   b.   In general, traditional methods of allocating overhead costs (including the use of departmental rates) will distort product costs when products differ in complexity, volume and how many units are in a batch.

D. Study the example of activity-based costing in Exhibit 3-3. Activity-based costing is just like the methods for applying overhead to products as described in Chapter 2. The only difference is that activity-based costing uses many overhead cost pools and rates rather than just one. The manufacturing overhead applied to a product in activity-based costing is determined as follows:

1. For each activity cost pool in turn, compute its activity rate (i.e., predetermined overhead rate) by dividing its estimated overhead cost by its expected activity.

2. For each activity cost pool in turn, multiply its activity rate by the activity required for each product. The result is the amount of cost for that activity cost pool that is applied to that product.

E.   The flow of costs through Raw Materials, Work In Process, and other accounts is basically the same under activity-based costing as shown in Chapter 2. The only difference is that more than one overhead rate is used to apply overhead to products under activity-based costing.

1. Using raw materials in production results in a debit to Work in Process and a credit to Raw Materials.

Work in Process	XXX	
Raw Materials		XXX

2. When direct labor costs are incurred, the debit is to Work in Process.

Work in Process	XXX	
Wages Payable		XXX

3. Actual manufacturing overhead costs are debited to Manufacturing Overhead as they are incurred.

Manufacturing Overhead	XXX	
Accounts Payable, Cash, etc.		XXX

4. Manufacturing overhead is applied to products based on the activities they require. If a product requires three purchase orders and two machine set-ups, it is charged for those purchase orders and machine set-ups using the activity rates for those activity cost pools. The manufacturing overhead applied is debited to Work in Process and credited to Manufacturing Overhead as they are incurred.

Work in Process	XXX	
Manufacturing Overhead		XXX

5. At the end of the period, the total actual manufacturing overhead incurred is compared to the total manufacturing overhead applied. If the amount applied exceeds the amount incurred, the overhead is overapplied. If the amount incurred exceeds the amount applied, the overhead is underapplied. Appropriate adjustments are then made to Cost of Goods Sold as discussed in Chapter 2.

REVIEW AND SELF-TEST
Questions and Exercises

True or False

For each of the following statements, enter a T or an F in the blank to indicate whether the statement is true or false.

___T___ 1. If direct labor is the allocation base for assigning overhead costs to products and direct labor does not cause overhead costs, the result will be distorted product costs.

___T___ 2. The key concept underlying activity-based costing is that products cause activities that consume resources and consumption of resources results in costs.

___T___ 3. Batch-level activities include issuing purchase orders, issuing production orders, and performing machine setups.

___F___ 4. Maintaining parts inventories is a unit-level activity.

___F___ 5. When activity-based costing is used, a company will have only one predetermined overhead rate.

___F___ 6. Overhead is neither underapplied nor overapplied when activity-based costing is used.

___F___ 7. Ordinarily, the unit product costs of high-volume products increase and the unit product costs of low-volume products decrease when activity-based costing replaces a traditional overhead costing systems based on direct labor-hours.

___T___ 8. When overhead is applied to a product, Work in Process is debited and Manufacturing Overhead is credited.

Multiple Choice

Choose the best answer or response by placing the identifying letter in the space provided.

___b___ 1. Issuing a purchase order is a: a) unit-level activity; b) batch-level activity; c) product-level activity; d) facility-level activity.

___D___ 2. Paying rent on a plant building is: a) a unit-level activity; b) a batch-level activity; c) a product-level activity; d) a facility-level activity.

___C___ 3. Testing the prototype of a new product is: a) a unit-level activity; b) a batch-level activity; c) a product-level activity; d) a facility-level activity.

___b___ 4. A company has two activity cost pools—machine setups and production orders. The total cost in the machine setup activity cost pool is $200,000 and the total cost in the production orders cost pool is $80,000. The estimated activity is 20,000 setups and 5,000 production orders. What is the activity rate for the machine setup activity cost pool? a) $16 per setup; b) $10 per setup; c) $56 per setup; d) $14 per setup.

___d___ 5. A company that provides photocopying services has an activity-based costing system with three activity cost pools—making photocopies, serving customers, and setting up machines. The activity rates are $0.02 per photocopy, $2.15 per customer, and $0.75 per machine-setup. If a customer requires set-ups on two different machines and makes 200 copies in total, how much overhead cost would be assigned to the job by the activity-based costing system? a) $4.00; b) $2.15; c) $1.50; d) $7.65.

Exercises

3-1.   Activity cost pools that might be found in a company using activity-based costing are listed below. For each activity, place an X under the proper heading to indicate whether the activity would be unit-level, batch-level, and so forth.

	Activity Cost Pool	Unit-Level Activity	Batch-Level Activity	Product-Level Activity	Facility Level Activity
a.	Manage parts inventory			X	
b.	Assemble products	X			
c.	Use factory building				X
d.	Issue purchase orders		X		
e.	Process products on machines	X			
f.	Heat the factory building				X
g.	Test product prototypes			X	
h.	Issue production orders		X		
i.	Design products			X	
j.	Set up machines		X		
k.	Run personnel department				X

3-2.   Kozales Company uses activity-based costing to compute unit product costs for external financial reports. The company manufactures two products—the Regular Model and the Super Model. During the coming year the company expects to produce 20,000 units of the Regular Model and 5,000 units of the Super Model. Other selected data relating to the coming year are listed below. Compute the overhead cost per unit for each product by filling in the missing data in the schedules provided.

Basic Data

Activity Cost Pool (and Activity Measure)	Estimated Overhead Costs	Regular	Super	Total
Labor related (direct labor-hours)	$ 80,000	8,000	2,000	10,000
Machine setups (number of setups)	420,000	500	900	1,400
Product testing (number of tests)	600,000	6,400	1,600	8,000
General factory (machine-hours)	900,000	30,000	15,000	45,000
Total manufacturing overhead cost	$2,000,000			

Header over Regular/Super/Total: *Expected Activity*

Overhead Rates by Activity Center

Activity Center	(a) Estimated Overhead Costs	(b) Expected Activity	(a) ÷ (b) Activity Rate
Labor related	$80,000	10,000 DLHs	$____8____ per __hour__
Machine setups...................	$420,000	1,400 setups	$__300__ per __Setup__
Product testing...................	$600,000	8,000 tests	$__75__ per __Unit Test__
General factory...................	$900,000	45,000 MHs	$__20__ per __MHs__

Overhead Cost per Unit

		Regular Product Activity	Regular Product Amount	Super Product Activity	Super Product Amount
Labor related, at ____8____		8000	64,000	2,000	16000
Machine setups, at __300__		500	150000	900	270000
Product testing, at __75__		6400	480000	1600	120000
General factory, at __20__		30,000	600000	15,000	300000
Total overhead cost assigned (a)			1294000		706000
Number of units produced (b)			20,000		5000
Overhead cost per unit (a) ÷ (b)			64.90		141.20

3-3.   Lawson Company uses activity-based costing to compute product costs for external reports. The company has three activity centers and applies overhead using the activity rates for the various activity cost pools. Data for the current year are presented below for the three activity cost pools:

Activity Cost Pools (and Activity Measures)	Estimated Overhead Cost	Expected Activity	Actual Activity
Batch setups (setups)..........................	$ 52,900	2,300	2,260
Material handling (loads)	100,800	2,800	2,770
General factory (DLHs).......................	65,000	2,500	2,440
Total manufacturing overhead cost	$218,700		

a.   Determine how much total overhead was applied to products during the year by filling in the missing data in the schedules that have been provided below.

Activity Cost Pool	Estimated Overhead Cost	Expected Activity	Activity Rate
Batch setups	$52,900	2,300	23
Material handling	$100,800	2,800	36
General factory.................	$65,000	2,500	26

Activity Cost Pool	Activity Rate	Actual Activity	Overhead Applied
Batch setups	23	2,260	51980
Material handling	36	2,770	99720
General factory..................	26	2,440	63440
Total overhead applied.......			215140

b.   Actual manufacturing overhead costs for the year were $216,860. Determine the overapplied or underapplied overhead by filling in the missing data in the table provided below. (Be sure to clearly label whether the overhead was overapplied or underapplied.)

Actual manufacturing overhead costs incurred	216860
Manufacturing overhead costs applied..................................	215140
Manufacturing overhead under applied.............................	1720

Answers to Questions and Exercises

True or False

1. T   If overhead is assigned based on direct labor rather on the bases that actually cause the overhead, product costs will be distorted.

2. T   This is the key concept underlying activity-based costing.

3. T   These activities are batch-level since they are required every time a batch is initiated.

4. F   This ordinarily a product-level activity.

5. F   Under activity-based costing, a company will have a predetermined overhead rate for each activity center.

6. F   Actual manufacturing overhead will seldom exactly equal manufacturing overhead applied even under activity-based costing.

7. F   Ordinarily, activity-based costing shifts costs from high-volume to low-volume products.

8. T   Applying overhead to a product involves debiting Work in Process and crediting Manufacturing Overhead.

Multiple Choice

1. b   See Exhibit 3-2.

2. d   See Exhibit 3-2.

3. c   See Exhibit 3-2.

4. b $200,000 ÷ 20,000 setups = $10 per setup

5. d   The costs would be assigned as follows:

Making photocopies (200 copies @ $0.02)	$4.00
Setting up machines (2 set-ups @ $0.75)	1.50
Serving customers (1 customer @ $2.15)	2.15
Total cost	$7.65

Exercises

3-1.

	Activity	Unit-Level Activity	Batch-Level Activity	Product-Level Activity	Facility Level Activity
a.	Manage parts inventory			X	
b.	Assemble products	X			
c.	Use factory building				X
d.	Issue purchase orders		X		
e.	Process products on machines	X			
f.	Heat the factory building				X
g.	Test product prototypes			X	
h.	Issue production orders		X		
i.	Design products			X	
j.	Set up machines		X		
k.	Run personnel department				X

3-2.
Overhead Rates by Activity Center

Activity Cost Pool	(a) Estimated Overhead Cost	(b) Expected Activity	(a) ÷ (b) Activity Rate
Labor related	$80,000	10,000 DLHs	$8.00 per DLH
Machine setups...................	$420,000	1,400 setups	$300.00 per setup
Product testing....................	$600,000	8,000 tests	$75.00 per test
General factory...................	$900,000	45,000 MHs	$20.00 per MH

Overhead Cost per Unit

	Regular Product		Super Product	
	Activity	Amount	Activity	Amount
Labor related, at $8 per DLH........................	8,000	$ 64,000	2,000	$ 16,000
Machine setups, at $300 per setup	500	150,000	900	270,000
Product testing, at $75 per test.....................	6,400	480,000	1,600	120,000
General factory, at $20 per MH	30,000	600,000	15,000	300,000
Total overhead cost assigned (a)...................		$1,294,000		$706,000
Number of units produced (b).......................		20,000		5,000
Overhead cost per unit (a) ÷ (b)...................		$64.70		$141.20

3-3.   a.   The first step is to compute the predetermined overhead rate for each activity center:

Activity Cost Pool	Estimated Overhead Cost	Expected Activity	Activity Rate
Batch setups	$52,900	2,300 setups	$23 per setup
Material handling	$100,800	2,800 loads	$36 per load
General factory.................	$65,000	2,500 DLHs	$26 per DLH

The amount of overhead applied to production is determined as follows:

Activity Cost Pool	Activity Rate	Actual Activity	Overhead Applied
Batch setups	$23 per setup	2,260 setups	$ 51,980
Material handling	$36 per load	2,770 loads	99,720
General factory.................	$26 per DLH	2,440 DLHs	63,440
Total overhead applied.....			$215,140

b.   Overhead was underapplied by $1,720.

Actual manufacturing overhead costs incurred	$216,860
Manufacturing overhead costs applied........................	215,140
Manufacturing overhead underapplied........................	$ 1,720

33

Chapter 4

Systems Design: Process Costing

Chapter Study Suggestions

The chapter is divided into four main parts. The first part compares job-order and process costing. Exhibit 4-1 outlines the differences between the two costing methods. The second part of the chapter covers cost flows in a process costing system. Study Exhibit 4-3 carefully, as well as the journal entries that follow. The third part of the chapter deals with a concept known as equivalent units of production. Pay particular attention to the computations in Exhibits 4-5 and 4-6.

The fourth part of the chapter shows how to prepare a production report using the weighted-average method. The production report is complex and you will need to devote a large portion of your time to learning how it is constructed. Exhibit 4-9 provides a detailed example of a production report.

CHAPTER HIGHLIGHTS

A. Process costing is used in industries that produce homogeneous products such as bricks, flour, and cement on a continuous basis.

B. Process costing is similar to job-order costing in three ways:

1. Both systems have the same basic purposes, which are to assign material, labor, and overhead costs to products and to provide a mechanism for computing unit costs.

2. Both systems use the same basic manufacturing accounts: Manufacturing Overhead, Raw Materials, Work in Process, and Finished Goods.

3. Costs flow through these accounts in basically the same way in both systems.

C. Process costing differs from job-order costing in three ways:

1. Costs are accumulated by department, rather than by job.

2. The department production report (rather than the job cost sheet) is the key document for recording costs.

3. Unit costs are computed by department (rather than by job). This computation is made on the department production report.

D. A *processing department* is any work center where materials, labor, or overhead costs are added. Processing departments in process costing have two common features. First, the activity carried out in the department is performed uniformly on all units passing through it. And second, the output of the department is basically homogeneous.

E. Less effort is usually required to use a process costing system than a job-order costing system; costs only need to be traced to a few processing departments rather than to many individual jobs.

F. Exhibit 4-3 provides a T-account model of cost flows in a process costing system. A separate work in process account is maintained for each processing department. Materials, labor, and overhead costs are entered directly into each processing department's work in process account.

G. Once costs have been totaled for a department, the department's output must be determined so that unit costs can be computed. Units that have only been partially completed pose a problem. A unit that is only 10% complete should not count as much as a unit that

has been completed and transferred on to the next department.

1. *Equivalent units* are the number of whole, complete units one could obtain from the materials or effort contained in completed and partially completed units. Equivalent units are computed using the following formula:

$$\begin{array}{c} \text{Equivalent} \\ \text{units} \end{array} = \begin{array}{c} \text{Number of partially} \\ \text{completed units} \end{array} \times \begin{array}{c} \text{Percentage} \\ \text{completion} \end{array}$$

2. The *equivalent units of production* is used to compute the cost per equivalent unit. Under the weighted-average method, the equivalent units of production are determined as follows:

Units completed and transferred out	XXX
+ Equivalent units in ending inventory	XXX
= Equivalent units of production	XXX

H. A separate cost per equivalent unit figure is computed within each processing department for each cost category. The cost categories may include:

1. Costs of prior departments associated with units transferred into the department.

2. Materials costs added in the department.

3. Direct labor costs added in the department.

4. Manufacturing overhead costs applied to the department.

In process costing, direct labor costs and manufacturing overhead costs are often combined into one cost category called *conversion costs*.

I. Note the following points concerning process costing:

1. The equivalent units of production and cost per equivalent unit must be computed for each cost category.

2. Units transferred out of the department to the next department—or, in the case of the last department, to finished goods—are considered to be 100% complete with respect to the work done by the transferring department.

3. The first processing department will not have a cost category for the costs of units transferred in, but subsequent departments will have such a cost category. Units in process in a department are considered to be 100% complete with respect to the costs of the prior department.

J. The purpose of the *production report* is to summarize all of the production activity that takes place in a department for a period. A production report has three parts:

   1. A *quantity schedule*, which shows the flow of units through the department, and the computation of equivalent units for each cost category for the period.

   2. A statement showing computation of the *cost per equivalent unit* for each cost category for the period.

   3. A *reconciliation* of all cost flows into and out of the department during the period.

Note: It would be a good idea to refer to Exhibit 4-9 as you go through the explanation of the production report below.

K. The purpose of the *quantity schedule* on the production report is to show the flow of units through a department. The schedule shows the number of units to be accounted for in a department and it shows how those units have been accounted for.

   1. The format of the quantity schedule under the weighted-average method is:

Units to be accounted for:	
Work in process, beginning	XXX
Started into production	XXX
Total units to be accounted for	XXX
Units accounted for as follows:	
Transferred out to the next	
department or to finished goods	XXX
Work in process, ending	XXX
Total units accounted for	XXX

   2. The equivalent units for the units transferred out and for the ending work in process inventory are listed next to the quantity schedule on the production report.

L. The second step in preparing a production report is to compute the *cost per equivalent unit* for each cost category. Under the weighted-average method, this involves summing the costs from the beginning inventory with any costs added during the period to arrive at total cost. This amount is then divided by the equivalent units of production for the cost category to determine the cost per equivalent unit.

M. The final step in a production report is to prepare a *reconciliation* of all costs. Costs are accounted for as either transferred out during the period or assigned to the ending work in process inventory. Costs are determined as follows:

   1. Units transferred out. These units are presumed to be 100% complete. (If they were not complete with respect to the work done in the department, they would not be transferred out.) The costs of units transferred out are computed by multiplying the number of units transferred out by the cost per equivalent unit for each cost category. These costs are then summed.

   2. Units in ending work in process inventory. Within each cost category, the number of equivalent units is multiplied by the cost per equivalent unit for that cost category. These costs are then summed.

N. Study Exhibit 4-9 carefully; which shows how the weighted-average method works. Note that this method combines costs from the beginning inventory with costs from the current period. It is called the weighted-average method because it averages together costs from the prior period with costs of the current period.

REVIEW AND SELF-TEST
Questions and Exercises

True or False

Enter a T or an F in the blank to indicate whether the statement is true or false.

__T__ 1. A company that makes a homogeneous product such wooden safety matches would typically use a process costing system.

__F__ 2. Under process costing it is important to identify the materials, labor, and overhead costs associated with a particular customer's order just as under job-order costing.

__T__ 3. In a process costing system, the production report replaces the job cost sheet.

__F__ 4. Costing is more difficult in a process costing system than in a job-order costing system.

__T__ 5. In a process costing system, a work in process account is maintained for each processing department.

__F__ 6. Since costs are accumulated by department in a process costing system, there is no need for a finished goods inventory account.

__F__ 7. In process costing, costs incurred in a department are not transferred to the next department.

__T__ 8. If beginning work in process inventory contains 500 units that are 60% complete, then the inventory contains 300 equivalent units.

Multiple Choice

Choose the best answer or response by placing the identifying letter in the space provided.

__a__ 1. The Mixing Department of Deerdon Company started 4,800 units into process during the month. Five hundred units were in the beginning inventory and 300 units were in the ending inventory. How many units were completed and transferred out during the month? a) 5,000; b) 4,600; c) 5,300; d) 5,100.

__a__ 2. Last month the Welding Department of Eager Company started 8,000 units into production. The department had 2,000 units in process at the beginning of the month that were 60% complete with respect to conversion costs, and 3,000 units in process at the end of the month that were 30% complete with respect to conversion costs. A total of 7,000 units were completed and transferred to the next department during the month. Using the weighted-average method, the equivalent units of production for conversion costs for the month would be: a) 7,900; b) 8,500; c) 9,200; d) 9,500.

____ 3. At the beginning of the month, 200 units were in process in the Stamping Department of Farwest Industrials Inc. and they were 70% complete with respect to materials. During the month 2,000 units were transferred to the next department. At the end of the month, 100 units were still in process and they were 60% complete with respect to materials. The materials cost in the beginning work in process inventory was $2,721 and $39,200 of materials costs were added during the month. Using the weighted-average method, what is the cost per equivalent unit for materials costs? a) $19.06; b) $20.35; c) $20.42; d) $19.60.

____ 4. The Weaving Department of Dolly Company had $8,000 of conversion cost in its beginning work in process inventory and added $64,000 of conversion cost during the month. The department completed 37,000 units during the month and had 10,000 units in the ending work in process inventory that were 30% complete as to conversion cost. Using the weighted-average method, the amount of cost assigned to the units in ending inventory would be: a) $12,600; b) $4,800; c) $11,200; d) $5,400.

____ 5. The Heat Treatment Department at Northern Pipe is the third department in a sequential process. The work in process account for the department would consist of: a) costs transferred in from the prior department; b) materials costs added in the Heat Treatment Department; c) conversion costs added in the Heat Treatment Department; d) all of the above.

Exercises

4-1.   Diebold Company has a process costing system. Data relating to activities in the Mixing Department for March follow:

	Units	Percent Completed Materials	Percent Completed Conversion
Work in process, March 1	5,000	100%	60%
Units started into production	80,000		
Work in process, March 31	2,000	100%	50%

All materials are added at the start of processing in the Mixing Department.

Using the weighted-average method, fill in the following quantity schedule and a computation of equivalent units for the month:

Quantity
Schedule

Units to be accounted for:

Work in process, beginning

(materials 100% complete;

conversion _60_ % complete)........................... 5000

Started into production 80,000

Total units to be accounted for 85000

		Equivalent Units Materials	Equivalent Units Conversion

Units accounted for as follows:

Transferred out during the month............................. 83000   83000   83000

Work in process, ending

(materials 100% complete;

conversion _50_ % complete)........................... 2000   2000   1000

Total units accounted for 85000   85000   84000

Chapter 4

4-2.   Minden Company uses the weighted-average method in its process costing system. Complete the cost reconciliation section of the production report below for the Welding Department, the first processing department in the company.

Production Report, Welding Department

Quantity schedule and equivalent units

	Quantity Schedule
Units to be accounted for:	
Work in process, beginning (materials 100% complete, labor and overhead 20% complete)	5,000
Started into production	75,000
Total units accounted for...................................	80,000

	Quantity Schedule	Equivalent Units		
		Materials	Labor	Overhead
Units accounted for as follows:				
Transferred out	72,000	72,000	72,000	72,000
Work in process, ending (materials 100% complete, labor and overhead 75% complete)	8,000	8,000	6,000	6,000
Total units accounted for	80,000	80,000	78,000	78,000

Costs per equivalent unit

	Total Cost	Materials	Labor	Overhead	Whole Unit
Cost to be accounted for:					
Work in process, beginning	$ 9,500	$ 4,500	$ 3,000	$ 2,000	
Cost added by the department.......................	460,500	75,500	231,000	154,000	
Total cost (a)..	$470,000	$ 80,000	$234,000	$156,000	
Equivalent units of production (b)......................	80,000	78,000	78,000		
Cost per equivalent unit (a)÷(b)		$1.00 +	$3.00 +	$2.00 =	$6.00

Cost reconciliation

		Equivalent Units		
		Materials	Labor	Overhead
Cost accounted for as follows:				
Transferred out ..... 72000 X 6 .... 432000 $		72000	72000	72000
Work in process, ending:				
Materials...... 8000 X 1 8000		8000		
Labor .... 6000 X 3 18000			6000	
Overhead ..... 6000 X 2 12000				6000
Total work in process, ending........................ _____				
Total cost accounted for ....$ 470,000				

Answers to Questions and Exercises

True or False

1. T   Process costing is often used by companies that make homogeneous products.

2. F   Since units are indistinguishable from each other, there is no need to identify costs by customer order.

3. T   See the discussion in Exhibit 4-1.

4. F   Costing is usually easier in a process costing system since material and labor costs do not have to be traced to individual jobs.

5. T   In a process costing system a work in process inventory account is maintained for each department. A production report is also prepared for each department.

6. F   A finished goods inventory account is needed in a process costing system for unsold finished units, just as in a job-order costing system.

7. F   As units move from one department to another, the costs that have been incurred to that point are transferred forward with the units.

8. T   500 units × 60% = 300 equivalent units.

Multiple Choice

1. a

Beginning inventory	500
Add units started into process	4,800
Total units	5,300
Less ending inventory	300
Completed and transferred	5,000

2. a

Units completed and transferred	7,000
Work in process, ending:	
3,000 units × 30%	900
Equivalent units of production	7,900

3. b

Cost in beginning work in process	$ 2,721
Cost added during the month	39,200
Total cost (a)	$41,921
Units transferred out	2,000
Equivalent units in ending	
work in process inventory	
(100 × 60%)	60
Equivalent units (b)	2,060
Cost per EU (a) ÷ (b)	$20.35

4. d

Cost in beginning work in process	$ 8,000
Cost added during the year	64,000
Total cost (a)	$72,000
Units transferred out	37,000
Equivalent units in ending	
work in process inventory	
(10,000 × 30%)	3,000
Equivalent units (b)	40,000
Cost per EU (a) ÷ (b)	$1.80

3,000 units × $1.80 = $5,400.

5. d   Costs in the department's work in process inventory account include costs transferred in from the previous department and any costs added in the department itself—including materials, labor, and overhead. Labor and overhead together equal conversion cost.

Exercises

4-1.

	Quantity Schedule		
Units to be accounted for:			
Work in process, beginning (materials 100% complete; conversion 60% complete).........................	5,000		
Started into production	80,000		
Total units to be accounted for	85,000		

		Equivalent Units	
		Materials	Conversion
Units accounted for as follows:			
Transferred out during the month....................	83,000	83,000	83,000
Work in process, ending (materials 100% complete; conversion 50% complete).........................	2,000	2,000	1,000
Total units accounted for	85,000	85,000	84,000

4-2.

	Total Cost	Equivalent Units		
		Materials	Labor	Overhead
Cost accounted for as follows:				
Transferred out:				
(72,000 units × $6 per unit)........................	$432,000	72,000	72,000	72,000
Work in process, ending:				
Materials cost ($1 per EU).........................	8,000	8,000		
Labor cost ($3 per EU)	18,000		6,000	
Overhead cost ($2 per EU)	12,000			6,000
Total work in process, ending.........................	38,000			
Total cost accounted for	$470,000			

Chapter 5

Cost Behavior: Analysis and Use

Chapter Study Suggestions

Chapter 5 expands on the discussion of fixed and variable costs that was started in Chapter 2. In addition, the chapter introduces a new concept—mixed costs—and shows how mixed costs can be separated into their fixed and variable elements. Focus the bulk of your study time on the section titled "The Analysis of Mixed Costs" that is found midway through the chapter. Pay particular attention to how a *cost formula* is derived and how a cost formula is used to predict future costs at various levels.

Memorize the elements of the equation $Y = a + bX$. You need to understand this equation to complete most of the homework exercises and problems. At the end of the chapter, a new format for the income statement is introduced that emphasizes cost behavior. Exhibit 5-13 illustrates the format of the contribution income statement. *This format should be memorized*—you will be using it throughout the rest of the book.

The appendix at the end of the chapter discusses variable costing and contrasts it to absorption costing.

CHAPTER HIGHLIGHTS

A. A *variable cost* is a cost that varies, in total, in proportion to changes in the level of activity. Variable costs are constant on a *per unit* basis.

　1. Activity is often measured in terms of the volume of goods produced or services provided by the organization. However, other measures of activity may be used for specific purposes such as patients admitted to a hospital, number of machinery setups performed, number of sales calls made, and so on.

　2. Exhibit 5-1 illustrates a variable cost. Note that a variable cost is a straight line that goes through zero (i.e., the origin) on the graph.

B. A *fixed cost* is a cost that remains constant in total within the relevant range. Fixed cost per unit varies inversely with changes in activity. As activity increases, per unit fixed costs fall.

　1. Fixed costs can be classified into committed and discretionary fixed costs.

　　a. *Committed fixed costs* relate to investments in facilities, equipment, and the basic organization of a company. These costs are difficult to adjust.

　　b. *Discretionary fixed costs* result from annual decisions by management to spend in certain areas, such as advertising, research, and management development programs. These costs are easier to modify than committed fixed costs.

　2. Even committed fixed costs may change if the change in activity is big enough. Exhibit 5-6 illustrates this idea. However, within the band of activity known as the relevant range, total fixed cost is constant.

C. A *mixed cost* (or semivariable cost) is a cost that contains both variable and fixed cost elements. Exhibit 5-7 illustrates a mixed cost.

　1. Examples of mixed costs include electricity, costs of processing bills, costs of admitting patients to a hospital, and maintenance.

　2. The fixed portion of a mixed cost represents the cost of providing capacity. The variable portion represents the additional cost of using the capacity.

D. The relevant range and curvilinear costs.

　1. For simplicity, a strict linear relation between cost and volume is usually assumed. However, many cost relationships are curvilinear, such as illustrated in Exhibit 5-4.

　2. The straight-line assumption is reasonable since any small portion of a curvilinear cost can be approximated by a straight line. The *relevant range* is the range of activity within which a particular straight line is a valid approximation to the curvilinear cost.

E. Cost formula for a mixed cost.

　1. The fixed and variable cost elements of a mixed cost can be expressed in a *cost formula*, which can be used to predict costs at all levels of activity within the relevant range. This formula is expressed as follows:

$$Y = a + bX$$
　where:
　　Y = *dependent variable* (the total mixed cost)
　　a = vertical intercept (the total fixed cost)
　　b = slope of the line (the variable cost)
　　X = *independent variable* (the activity level)

　2. Each of the methods discussed below can be used to estimate the variable cost per unit (b) and the total fixed cost (a) based on data from prior periods. Then with the use of the cost formula, the expected amount of total cost (Y) can be computed for any expected activity level (X) within the relevant range.

F. The analysis of a mixed cost begins with records of past cost and activity. The first step is to plot the cost and activity data on a *scattergraph*. The cost is represented on the vertical (Y) axis and activity is represented on the horizontal (X) axis.

　1. If the scattergraph plot indicates that the relation between cost and activity is approximately linear (i.e., a straight line), the analysis can proceed to the next stage of estimating the variable cost per unit of activity and the fixed cost per period.

　2. A quick and dirty way to estimate the variable and fixed costs is to draw a straight line on the scattergraph plot. The intercept of the line with the vertical axis is the estimated total fixed cost. The slope of the line is the estimated variable cost per unit of activity.

G. The *high-low method* estimates the variable and fixed elements of a mixed cost using only the data at the highest and lowest levels of activity.

　1. The high-low method uses a variation of the "rise over run" formula for the slope of a straight line. The change in cost observed between the two extremes is divided by the change in activity to estimate the amount of variable cost. The formula is:

$$\frac{\text{Variable cost}}{\text{per unit of activity}} = \frac{\text{Change in cost}}{\text{Change in activity}}$$

2. The estimated variable cost per unit of activity (i.e., variable rate) is then used to estimate the fixed cost as follows:

Total cost at the high activity level........	$XXX
Less variable portion:	
Variable rate × High activity level.....	XXX
Fixed portion of the mixed cost.............	$ XXX

3. The high-low method is quick, but is not reliable. It is based on costs and activity for only two periods—the periods with the highest and lowest levels of activity. Other data are ignored and these two periods tend to be unusual and may not be representative of typical cost behavior.

H. The *least-squares regression method* fits a line, called a *regression line*, to cost and activity data using a formula. The least-squares regression formula calculates the slope and intercept of the straight line that minimizes the sum of the squared errors from the regression line. The computations are fairly complex and are best carried out with the aid of statistical or spreadsheet application software.

I. The *contribution approach* to preparation of an income statement emphasizes cost behavior.

1. The *traditional format* for income statements groups expenses into functional categories:

Sales..	$XXX
Cost of goods sold	XXX
Gross margin	XXX
Selling and administrative expense..........	XXX
Net operating income..............................	$XXX

2. In contrast, the *contribution approach* groups expenses according to their cost behavior.

Sales..	$XXX
Less variable expenses.............................	XXX
Contribution margin	XXX
Less fixed expenses	XXX
Net operating income..............................	$XXX

3. Note that the *contribution margin* is determined by deducting variable expenses from sales.

4. The contribution approach is very useful in internal reports since it emphasizes the behavior of costs. As you will see in later chapters, this is very important in planning, budgeting, controlling operations, and in performance evaluation. However, in external reports the traditional format that emphasizes cost by function must be used.

Appendix 5A

A. Two different methods can be used to determine unit product costs—*absorption costing* and *variable costing.*

1. Under *absorption costing*, all manufacturing costs, both variable and fixed, are included in unit product costs.

Direct materials	$XXX
Direct labor	XXX
Variable manufacturing overhead	XXX
Fixed manufacturing overhead	XXX
Unit product cost	$XXX

2. Under *variable costing*, only variable manufacturing costs—which usually consist of direct materials, direct labor, and variable manufacturing overhead—are included in unit product costs.

Direct materials	$XXX
Direct labor	XXX
Variable manufacturing overhead	XXX
Unit product cost	$XXX

3. Under the variable costing method, fixed manufacturing costs are treated as period costs and are expensed in the period in which they are incurred, just like selling and administrative expenses.

B. Under absorption costing, fixed manufacturing costs may be shifted from one period to another due to changes in inventories.

1. A small portion of the period's fixed manufacturing overhead costs is assigned to each unit that is produced. If the unit is not sold during the period, the fixed manufacturing overhead assigned to the unit is part of the inventories on the balance sheet rather than cost of goods sold on the income statement. This is referred to as *deferral of fixed manufacturing overhead in inventory.*

2. Exhibit 5A-1 is a key exhibit illustrating the differences between variable and absorption costing. *Study this exhibit carefully before going on.*

C. Any difference in net operating income between variable and absorption costing can be traced to changes in the level of inventories.

1. When production and sales (in units) are equal and hence inventories don't change, both variable and absorption costing will yield the same net operating income.

2. When production exceeds sales (in units) and hence inventories increase, greater net operating income will be reported under absorption costing than under variable costing.

   a. When inventories increase, some of the current period's *fixed manufacturing overhead costs are deferred in inventory.*

   b. The amount of fixed manufacturing overhead cost deferred is equal to the increase in units in inventory multiplied by the fixed manufacturing overhead cost per unit.

3. When production is less than sales (in units) and hence inventories decrease, less net operating income will be reported under absorption costing than under variable costing.

    a. *Fixed manufacturing overhead costs are released from inventory* when the units in inventory are sold.

    b. The amount of fixed manufacturing overhead cost released is equal to the decrease in units in inventory multiplied by the fixed manufacturing overhead cost per unit.

4. Over an extended period of time, the net operating income reported by the two costing methods will tend to be the same. Over the long run sales can't exceed production, nor can production much exceed sales. The shorter the period, the more the net operating income figures will tend to differ.

D. The following form can be used to reconcile the variable costing and absorption costing net operating income figures.

Variable costing net operating income	$XXX
Add: Fixed manufacturing overhead costs deferred in inventory under absorption costing	XXX
Deduct: Fixed manufacturing overhead costs released from inventory under absorption costing	(XXX)
Absorption costing net operating income	$XXX

REVIEW AND SELF-TEST
Questions and Exercises

True or False

Enter a T or an F in the blank to indicate whether the statement is true or false.

__T__ 1. Variable costs are costs that change, in total, in proportion to changes in the activity level.

__F__ 2. In cost analysis work, activity is known as the dependent variable.

__T__ 3. Within the relevant range, the higher the activity level, the lower the fixed cost per unit.

__F__ 4. Contribution margin and gross margin mean the same thing.

__T__ 5. Contribution margin is the difference between sales and variable expenses.

__T__ 6. Discretionary fixed costs arise from annual decisions by management to spend in certain areas.

__F__ 7. Advertising is a committed fixed cost.

__F__ 8. A mixed cost is a cost that contains both manufacturing and non-manufacturing costs.

__T__ 9. Within the relevant range, the relation between cost and activity is approximately a straight line.

__F__ 10. In order for a cost to be variable, it must vary with either units produced or services provided.

__T__ 11. The contribution approach to the income statement organizes costs according to behavior, rather than according to function.

__F__ 12. (Appendix 5A) Product costs under the absorption costing method consist of direct materials, direct labor, and both variable and fixed manufacturing overhead.

__T__ 13. (Appendix 5A) Selling and administrative expenses are treated as period costs under both variable costing and absorption costing.

__F__ 14. (Appendix 5A) Variable costing will always produce higher net operating income than absorption costing.

__T__ 15. (Appendix 5A) When production exceeds sales, the net operating income reported under absorption costing will generally be greater than the net operating income reported under variable costing.

Multiple Choice

Choose the best answer or response by placing the identifying letter in the space provided.

__C__ 1. A company's cost formula for maintenance is $Y = \$4,000 + \$3X$, where X is machine-hours. During a period in which 2,000 machine-hours are worked, the expected maintenance cost would be: a) $12,000; b) $6,000; c) $10,000; d) $4,000.

__ __ 2. The costs associated with a company's basic facilities, equipment, and organization are known as: a) committed fixed costs; b) discretionary fixed costs; c) mixed costs; d) variable costs.

__D__ 3. Last year, Barker Company's sales were $240,000, its fixed costs were $50,000, and its variable costs were $2 per unit. During the year, 80,000 units were sold. The contribution margin was: a) $200,000; b) $240,000; c) $30,000; d) $80,000.

__ __ 4. An example of a discretionary fixed cost would be: a) depreciation on equipment; b) rent on a factory building; c) salaries of top management; d) items a, b, and c are all discretionary fixed costs; e) none of the above.

__b__ 5. In March, Espresso Express had electrical costs of $225.00 when the total volume was 4,500 cups of coffee served. In April, electrical costs were $227.50 for 4,750 cups of coffee. Using the high-low method, what is the estimated fixed cost of electricity per month? a) $200; b) $180; c) $225; d) $150.

__ __ 6. (Appendix 5A) White Company manufactures a single product and has the following cost structure:

Variable costs per unit:
Direct materials	$3
Direct labor	$4
Variable manufacturing overhead	$1
Variable selling and admin. expense......	$2
Fixed costs per month:	
Fixed manufacturing overhead $100,000	
Fixed selling & admin. Expense $60,000	

The company produces 20,000 units each month. The unit product cost under absorption costing is: a) $10; b) $13; c) $15; d) $12.

__ __ 7. (Appendix 5A) Refer to the data in question 6 above. The unit product cost under variable costing would be: a) $8; b) $10; c) $13; d) $11.

47

___ 8. (Appendix 5A) Refer to the data in question 6 above. Assume beginning inventories are zero, 20,000 units are produced, and 19,000 units are sold in a month. If the unit selling price is $20, what is the net operating income under absorption costing for the month? a) $30,000; b) $38,000; c) $35,000; d) $42,000.

___ 9. (Appendix 5A) Refer to the data in question 6 above. Assume beginning inventories are zero, and 20,000 units are produced, and 19,000 units are sold in a month. If the unit selling price is $20, what is the net operating income under variable costing for the month? a) $30,000; b) $38,000; c) $35,000; d) $42,000.

___ 10. (Appendix 5A) Refer to your answers to parts 8 and 9 above. The net operating income differs between variable and absorption costing in this situation because: a) variable costs are $5,000 higher under variable costing; b) $5,000 in fixed manufacturing overhead has been deferred in inventories under absorption costing; c) $5,000 in fixed manufacturing overhead has been released from inventories under absorption costing; d) none of the above.

___ 11. (Appendix 5A) Which of the following costs are treated as period costs under the variable costing method? a) fixed manufacturing overhead and both variable and fixed selling and administrative expenses; b) both variable and fixed manufacturing overhead; c) only fixed manufacturing overhead and fixed selling and administrative expenses.

___ 12. (Appendix 5A) When production exceeds sales, fixed manufacturing overhead costs: a) are released from inventory under absorption costing; b) are deferred in inventory under absorption costing; c) are released from inventory under variable costing; d) are deferred in inventory under variable costing.

___ 13. (Appendix 5A) When sales are constant but production fluctuates: a) net operating income will be erratic under variable costing; b) absorption costing will always show a net loss; c) variable costing will always show a positive net operating income; d) net operating income will be erratic under absorption costing.

Exercises

5-1.   Data concerning the electrical costs at Doughboy Company follow:

	Machine hours	Electrical cost
Week 1................	6,800 hrs.	$1,770
Week 2................	6,000 hrs.	1,650
Week 3................	5,400 hrs.	1,560
Week 4................	7,900 hrs.	1,935

a.   Plot the data on the following scattergraph:

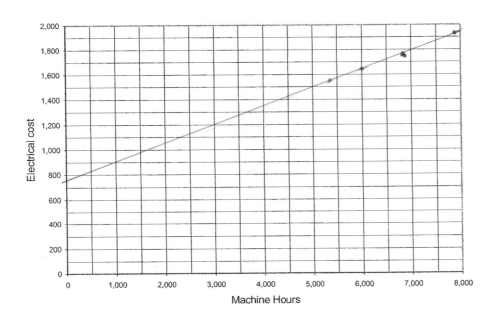

b.   Is the relation between machine-hours and electrical costs approximately linear? Explain.

_____

_____

_____

_____

Chapter 5

5-2.   Refer to the data for Doughboy in the previous exercise.

a.   Using the high-low method of cost analysis, what is the variable cost per machine-hour at Doughboy?

	Cost	Machine Hours
High activity level	1935	7900
Low activity level	1560	5400
Change	375	2500

$$\frac{\text{Change in cost}}{\text{Change in activity}} = \frac{375}{2500} = \$ \underline{0.15} \text{ per machine hour}$$

b.   Using the high-low method of cost analysis, what is the total fixed cost?

Total cost at the high activity level	1935
Less variable cost element:	
0.15 × 7900	1185
Fixed cost element	750

c.   Express the cost formula for electrical costs in the form Y = a + bX: $Y = 750 + 0.15X$

5-3. During July, Cramer's, Inc., a wholesale distributor of a unique software product, sold 500 units. The company's income statement for the month follows:

Cramer's, Inc.
Income Statement
For the Month Ended July 31

Sales ($100 per unit)		$50,000
Cost of goods sold ($60 per unit)		30,000
Gross margin		20,000
Selling and administrative expenses:		
Commissions ($6 per unit)	$3,000	
Salaries	8,000	
Advertising	6,000	
Shipping ($2 per unit)	1,000	18,000
Net operating income		$ 2,000

Redo the company's income statement for the month in the contribution format. Assume that cost of goods sold, commissions, and shipping expenses are variable costs and salaries and advertising expenses are fixed costs.

Cramer's, Inc.
Income Statement
For the Month Ended July 31

Sales		$ 50 000
Less Variable Exp :		
Cost of good sold (60X500)	$ 30,000	
Commi (6X500)	3000	
Ship (2x500)	1000	34000
Contribution margin		16,000
Less Fixed Exp. :		
Adv	6,000	
Salaries	8000	14000
Net operating income		$ 2000

51

5-4.   (Appendix 5A) Selected data relating to the operations of Dover Company for last year are given below:

Units in beginning inventory	0
Units produced	40,000
Units sold	35,000
Units in ending inventory	5,000
Selling price per unit	$27
Variable costs per unit:	
Direct materials	$7
Direct labor	$6
Variable manufacturing overhead	$3
Variable selling and administrative	$2
Fixed costs:	
Fixed manufacturing overhead	$160,000
Fixed selling and administrative	$140,000

a.   Assume that the company uses absorption costing.

Compute the unit product cost. .... $ _20_

Determine the value of the ending inventory. _5000×20_ .... $ ~~5000~~ ~~10,000~~ 100,000.

Complete the following absorption costing income statement:

Sales .... _27 y 35000_ .... $ 945000

Cost of goods sold 700000

Gross margin 245000

Selling and administrative expenses................ 210000

Net operating income .... $ 35000

b.   Assume that the company uses variable costing.

Compute the unit product cost. .... $___16___

Determine the value of the ending inventory. ...16 x 5000... $ 80,000

Complete the following contribution format income statement using variable costing:

Sales   ....35000 x 27............................... $ 945000

Less variable expenses:

Variable cost of goods sold 560000

Variable selling and administrative 70000   630000

Contribution margin 315000

Less fixed expenses:

Fixed manufacturing overhead 160000

Fixed selling and administrative 140000   300000

Net operating income .... $ 15,000

c.   Reconcile the net operating incomes under the two methods by filling in the following form:

Variable costing net operating income .... $_____
Add fixed manufacturing overhead cost deferred
    in inventory under absorption costing .... _____
Deduct fixed manufacturing overhead cost released
    from inventory under absorption costing .... _____

Absorption costing net operating income .... $_____

Answers to Questions and Exercises

True or False

1. **T** This is the definition of a variable cost.

2. **F** Activity is the independent variable.

3. **T** Fixed costs vary inversely with changes in activity when expressed on a per unit basis.

4. **F** Contribution margin is sales less variable expenses; gross margin is sales less cost of goods sold.

5. **T** This is true by definition.

6. **T** Discretionary fixed costs are re-evaluated each year by management.

7. **F** Advertising is a discretionary fixed cost since the advertising program is typically re-evaluated on an annual basis.

8. **F** Mixed costs contain both variable and fixed cost elements.

9. **T** By definition, a straight line is a reasonable approximation to the real cost behavior within a relevant range.

10. **F** Activity can be measured in many ways besides units produced and units sold. Other measures include miles driven, number of occupied beds in a hospital, and number of flight hours.

11. **T** The contribution approach groups variable costs together and fixed costs together; thus, the income statement is organized according to cost behavior.

12. **T** All manufacturing costs are included as product costs under absorption costing.

13. **T** Selling and administrative expenses are never treated as product costs under either costing method.

14. **F** Variable costing will produce higher net operating income than absorption costing only when sales exceed production.

15. **T** When production exceeds sales, fixed manufacturing overhead cost is deferred in inventory under absorption costing. Consequently, net operating income is higher under absorption costing than under variable costing.

Multiple Choice

1. **c**
Fixed cost	$ 4,000
Variable cost: $3 × 2,000 hours	6,000
Total cost	$10,000

2. **a** Committed fixed costs relate to basic facilities, equipment, and organization.

3. **d**
Sales	$240,000
Less variable costs:	
$2 × 80,000 units	160,000
Contribution margin	$ 80,000

4. **e** All of the listed costs are generally considered to be committed fixed costs.

5. **b**

	Cost	Cups
High activity level	$227.50	4,750
Low activity level	225.00	4,500
Change	$ 2.50	250

$$\frac{\text{Change in cost}}{\text{Change in activity}} = \frac{\$2.50}{250} = \$0.01 \text{ per cup}$$

Total cost at the high activity	$227.50
Less variable cost element:	
4,750 cups × $0.01 per cup	47.50
Fixed cost element	$180.00

6. **b**
Variable manufacturing costs ($3 + $4 + $1)	$ 8
Fixed manufacturing costs ($100,000 ÷ 20,000 units)	5
Unit product cost	$13

7. **a** Only the variable manufacturing costs are treated as product costs under variable costing. Thus, the unit product cost is $3 + $4 + $1 = $8.

8. **c** The absorption costing net operating income is computed as follows:

Sales	$380,000
Cost of goods sold	247,000
Gross margin	133,000
Selling & admin.	
Variable selling & admin.	38,000
Fixed selling & admin.	60,000
Total selling & admin.	98,000
Net operating income	$ 35,000

9. a   The variable costing net operating income is computed as follows:

Sales	$380,000
Less variable expenses:	
Variable cost of goods sold	152,000
Variable selling & admin.	38,000
Total variable expenses	190,000
Contribution margin	190,000
Less fixed expenses:	
Fixed manuf. overhead	100,000
Fixed selling & admin.	60,000
Total fixed expenses	160,000
Net operating income	$ 30,000

10. b   Inventories increased by 1,000 units. Under absorption costing, $5 (=$100,000 ÷ 20,000 units) of fixed manufacturing overhead cost is applied to each unit that is produced. Thus, $5,000 in fixed manufacturing overhead costs are deferred in inventories and do not appear on the income statement as part of cost of goods sold.

11. a   Fixed manufacturing overhead cost is expensed as incurred under variable costing. Also, both variable and fixed selling and administrative expenses are always treated as period costs under both variable and absorption costing.

12. b   When production exceeds sales, units are added to inventory. Thus, fixed manufacturing overhead costs are deferred in inventory under absorption costing.

13. d   When production fluctuates, net operating income will be erratic under absorption costing since fixed manufacturing overhead costs will be shifted into and out of inventory as production goes up and down.

Exercises

5-1. a. The scattergraph plot looks like this:

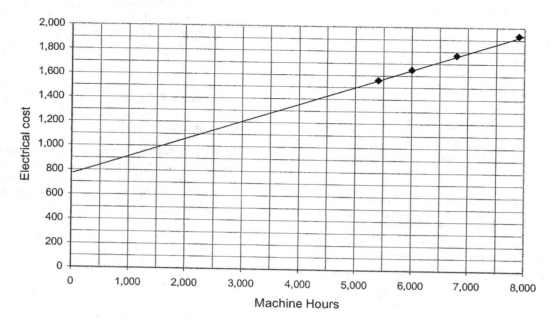

b. The relation between machine-hours and electrical costs is almost perfectly linear—a straight line can be drawn through all of the points on the scattergraph.

5-2. a. Variable cost per machine-hour:

		Machine
	Cost	Hours
High activity level	$1,935	7,900
Low activity level	1,560	5,400
Change	$ 375	2,500

$$\frac{\text{Change in cost}}{\text{Change in activity}} = \frac{\$375}{2{,}500 \text{ hours}} = \$0.15 \text{ per machine hour}$$

b. Total fixed cost:

Total cost at the high activity level	$1,935
Less variable cost element:	
7,900 hours × $0.15 per hour	1,185
Fixed cost element	$ 750

c. Cost formula for electrical costs: $750 per period, plus $0.15 per machine-hour, or
Y= $750 + $0.15X

5-3.

Cramer's, Inc.
Income Statement
For the Month Ended July 31

Sales ($100 per unit)...		$50,000
Less variable expenses:		
Cost of goods sold ($60 per unit)	$30,000	
Commissions ($6 per unit)	3,000	
Shipping ($2 per unit).................................	1,000	34,000
Contribution margin		16,000
Less fixed expenses:		
Salaries	8,000	
Advertising..	6,000	14,000
Net operating income		$ 2,000

5-4.   a.

Direct materials	$ 7
Direct labor...	6
Variable manufacturing overhead	3
Fixed manufacturing overhead ($160,000 ÷ 40,000 units)..............	4
Unit product cost	$20
Ending inventory (5,000 units × $20 per unit)	$100,000

Absorption costing income statement

Sales (35,000 units × $27 per unit)...	$945,000
Cost of goods sold (35,000 units × $20 per unit)	700,000
Gross margin	245,000
Selling & admin. expenses [(35,000 units × $2 per unit) + $140,000]..............	210,000
Net operating income	$ 35,000

b.

Direct materials	$ 7
Direct labor..	6
Variable manufacturing overhead	3
Unit product cost	$16
Ending inventory (5,000 units × $16 per unit)	$80,000

Variable costing income statement

Sales (35,000 units × $27 per unit)...........................		$945,000
Less variable expenses:		
Variable cost of goods sold (35,000 units × $16 per unit)...	$560,000	
Variable selling & admin. (35,000 units × $2 per unit).......	70,000	630,000
Contribution margin		315,000
Less fixed expenses:		
Fixed manufacturing overhead............................	160,000	
Fixed selling and administrative	140,000	300,000
Net operating income		$ 15,000

c. Reconciliation of variable costing and absorption costing net operating incomes:

Variable costing net operating income	$15,000
Add fixed manufacturing overhead cost deferred in inventory under absorption costing (5,000 units × $4 per unit)	20,000
Deduct fixed manufacturing overhead cost released from inventory under absorption costing	0
Absorption costing net operating income	$35,000

Chapter 6

Cost-Volume-Profit Relationships

Chapter Study Suggestions

Chapter 6 is one of the key chapters in the book. Many of the chapters ahead depend on concepts developed here. You should study several sections in the chapter with particular attention. The first of these is the section titled, "Contribution Margin." Note how changes in the contribution margin affect net operating income. The next section you should study with particular care is titled "Contribution Margin Ratio." The contribution margin ratio is used in much of the analytical work in the chapter.

Another section you should study very carefully is titled "Some Applications of CVP Concepts." Much of the homework material is drawn from this section. The section titled "Break-Even Analysis" also forms the basis for much of the homework material. Finally, the section titled "The Concept of Sales Mix" shows how to use CVP analysis when there is more than one product.

When studying the material in the chapter, try especially hard to understand the logic behind the solutions.

CHAPTER HIGHLIGHTS

A. The contribution margin is a key concept that will be used throughout the chapter and in subsequent chapters.

1. The contribution margin is the difference between total sales and total variable expenses:

Sales	XXX
Less variable expenses	XXX
Contribution margin	XXX

2. The unit contribution margin is the difference between the unit selling price and the unit variable expenses:

Selling price per unit	XXX
Less variable expenses per unit	XXX
Unit contribution margin	XXX

3. The relation between the contribution margin and the unit contribution margin is simple. The contribution margin is equal to the unit contribution margin multiplied by the number of units sold:

Unit contribution margin	XXX
× Unit sales	XXX
Contribution margin	XXX

4. Net operating income is equal to the contribution margin less fixed expenses.

Sales	XXX
Less variable expenses	XXX
Contribution margin	XXX
Less fixed expenses	XXX
Net operating income	XXX

5. The *break-even point* is the sales at which profits are zero. This occurs when the total contribution margin just equals fixed expenses.

6. The relation between contribution margin and net operating income provides a very powerful planning tool. It gives the manager the ability to predict what profits will be at various activity levels without the necessity of preparing detailed income statements.

   a. The contribution margin must first cover fixed expenses. If it doesn't, there is a loss. Below the break-even point, every unit sold reduces the loss by the amount of the unit contribution margin.

   b. Once the break-even point is reached, net operating income will increase by the amount of the unit contribution margin for each additional unit sold.

B. The contribution margin ratio (CM ratio), which expresses the contribution margin as a percentage of sales, is another very powerful concept.

1. The contribution margin ratio can be computed as follows:

$$\text{CM ratio} = \frac{\text{Contribution margin}}{\text{Sales}}$$

Or, if the company has only a single product:

$$\text{CM ratio} = \frac{\text{Unit contribution margin}}{\text{Unit selling price}}$$

2. The contribution margin ratio is used to predict the change in total contribution margin that would result from a given change in dollar sales:

Change in dollar sales	XXX
× CM ratio	XXX
Change in contribution margin	XXX

3. If fixed expenses do not change, any increase (or decrease) in contribution margin will be reflected dollar-for-dollar in increased (or decreased) net operating income.

4. The CM ratio is particularly useful when a company has multiple products since the CM ratio is expressed in terms of total dollar sales, which provides a useful common denominator.

C. Cost-volume-profit (CVP) concepts can be used in many day-to-day decisions. Carefully study the examples given under the heading "Some Applications of CVP Concepts" in the chapter.

1. Notice that each solution makes use of either the unit contribution margin or the CM ratio. This underscores the importance of these two concepts.

2. Also notice that several of the examples employ *incremental analysis*. An incremental analysis is based only on costs and revenues that *differ* between alternatives.

D. Two particular examples of CVP analysis are called *break-even analysis* and *target profit analysis*.

1. Target profit analysis is used to determine how much the company would have to sell to attain a specific target profit. The analysis is based on the following equation:

Profits = (Sales – Variable expenses) – Fixed expenses

In CVP analysis, this equation is often rewritten in the following format:

Sales = Variable expenses + Fixed expenses + Profits

All of the problems can be worked using this basic equation and simple algebra. However, handy formulas are available for answering some of the more common questions. These formulas are discussed below.

2. Target profit analysis is used in two basic variations. In the first variation, the question is how many *units* would have to be sold to attain the target profit. In the second variation, the question is how much total *dollar sales* would have to be to attain the target profit. The formulas are:

$$\frac{\text{Units sold to}}{\text{attain target profit}} = \frac{\text{Fixed expenses} + \text{Target profit}}{\text{Unit contribution margin}}$$

$$\frac{\text{Dollar sales to}}{\text{attain target profit}} = \frac{\text{Fixed expenses} + \text{Target profit}}{\text{CM ratio}}$$

E. Break-even occurs when profit is zero. Thus, break-even analysis is really just a special case of target profit analysis in which the target profit is zero. Therefore, the break-even formulas can be stated as follows:

$$\frac{\text{Breakeven point}}{\text{in units sold}} = \frac{\text{Fixed expenses}}{\text{Unit contribution margin}}$$

$$\frac{\text{Breakeven point}}{\text{in total sales dollars}} = \frac{\text{Fixed expenses}}{\text{CM ratio}}$$

F. CVP and break-even analysis can also be done graphically. Exhibits 6-1 and 6-2 show how a CVP graph is prepared and interpreted. A cost-volume-profit graph shows the relations among sales, costs, and volume throughout wide ranges of activity.

G. The *margin of safety* is the excess of budgeted (or actual) sales over the break-even volume of sales. It is the amount by which sales can drop before losses begin to be incurred. The margin of safety can be stated in terms of either dollars or as a percentage of sales:

Total budgeted (or actual) sales	XXX
Less break-even sales...........................	XXX
Margin of safety.................................	XXX

$$\frac{\text{Margin of safety}}{\text{percentage}} = \frac{\text{Margin of safety}}{\text{Total budgeted (or actual) sales}}$$

H. A company's cost structure—the relative proportion of fixed and variable costs—has an impact on how sensitive the company's profits are to changes in sales. A company with low fixed costs and high variable costs will tend to have a lower CM ratio than a company with a greater proportion of fixed costs. Such a company will tend to have less volatile profits, but at the risk of losing substantial profits if sales increase.

I. *Operating leverage* refers to the effect changes in sales have on net operating income.

1. The degree of operating leverage is defined as:

$$\frac{\text{Degree of operating}}{\text{leverage}} = \frac{\text{Contribution margin}}{\text{Net operating income}}$$

2. A given *percentage* in sales is multiplied by the degree of operating leverage to estimate the resulting *percentage* change in net operating income.

Percentage change in dollar sales	XXX
× Degree of operating leverage	XXX
Percentage change in net operating income	XXX

3. *The degree of operating leverage is not constant.* It changes as sales increase or decrease. *The degree of operating leverage decreases the further a company moves away from its break-even point.*

J. When a company has more than one product, the *sales mix*, or proportions in which its products are sold, can be crucial.

1. When CVP analysis involves more than one product, the analysis is normally based on the *overall contribution margin ratio*. This is computed using overall figures for both the contribution margin and sales:

$$\text{Overall CM ratio} = \frac{\text{Overall contribution margin}}{\text{Overall sales}}$$

2. When the company has more than one product, the *overall* CM ratio is used in the target profit and break-even formulas instead of the CM ratio.

3. As the sales mix changes *the overall CM ratio will also change.* If the shift is toward less profitable products, then the overall CM ratio will fall; if the shift is toward more profitable products, then the overall CM ratio will rise.

K. CVP analysis ordinarily relies on the following assumptions:

1. The selling price is constant; it does not change as unit sales change.

2. Costs are linear. Costs can be accurately divided into variable and fixed elements. The variable cost per unit is constant and the total fixed cost is constant.

3. In multi-product situations, the sales mix is constant.

4. In manufacturing companies, inventories do not change.

REVIEW AND SELF-TEST
Questions and Exercises

True or False

Enter a T or an F in the blank to indicate whether the statement is true or false.

___F___ 1. If product A has a higher unit contribution margin than product B, then product A will also have a higher CM ratio than product B.

___F___ 2. The break-even point occurs where the contribution margin is equal to total variable expenses.

___T___ 3. The break-even point can be expressed either in terms of units sold or in terms of total sales dollars.

___T___ 4. If the sales mix changes, the break-even point may change.

___T___ 5. For a given increase in sales dollars, a high CM ratio will result in a greater increase in profits than will a low CM ratio.

___F___ 6. If sales increase by 8%, and the degree of operating leverage is 4, then profits can be expected to increase by 12%.

___F___ 7. The degree of operating leverage is the same at all levels of sales.

___T___ 8. Once the break-even point has been reached, net operating income will increase by the unit contribution margin for each additional unit sold.

___F___ 9. A shift in sales mix toward less profitable products will cause the overall break-even point to fall.

___T___ 10. Incremental analysis focuses on the differences in costs and revenues between alternatives.

___F___ 11. If a company's cost structure shifts toward greater fixed costs and lower variable costs, one would expect the company's CM ratio to fall.

___F___ 12. One way to compute the break-even point is to divide total sales by the CM ratio.

___T___ 13. When a company has more than one product, a key assumption in break-even analysis is that the sales mix will not change.

Multiple Choice

Choose the best answer or response by placing the identifying letter in the space provided.

____ 1. Lester Company has a single product. The selling price is $50 and the variable cost is $30 per unit. The company's fixed expenses are $200,000 per month. What is the company's unit contribution margin? a) $50; b) $30; c) $20; d) $80.

___b___ 2. Refer to the data for Lester Company in question 1 above. What is the company's contribution margin ratio? a) 0.60; b) 0.40; c) 1.67; d) 20.00.

___a___ 3. Refer to the data for Lester Company in question 1 above. What is the company's break-even in sales dollars? a) $500,000; b) $33,333; c) $200,000; d) $400,000.

___B___ 4. Refer to the data for Lester Company in question 1 above. How many units would the company have to sell to attain target profits of $50,000? a) 10,000; b) 12,500; c) 15,000; d) 13,333.

___C___ 5. The following amounts are taken from Parker Company's contribution margin income statement: Net operating income, $30,000; Fixed expenses, $90,000; Sales, $200,000; and CM ratio, 60%. The company's margin of safety in dollars is: a) $150,000; b) $30,000; c) $50,000; d) $80,000.

___D___ 6. Refer to the data in question for Parker Company in 5 above. The margin of safety in percentage form is: a) 60%; b) 75%; c) 40%; d) 25%.

___B___ 7. Refer to the data for Parker Company in question 5 above. What is the company's total contribution margin? a) $110,000; b) $120,000; c) $170,000; d) $200,000.

___D___ 8. Refer to the data for Parker Company in question 5 above. What is the company's degree of operating leverage? a) 0.25; b) 0.60; c) 1.25; d) 4.00.

___B___ 9. If a company's sales increase from $400,000 to $450,000, and if the company's degree of operating leverage is 6, net operating income should increase by: a) 12.5%; b) 75%; c) 67%; d) 50%.

___B___ 10. In multi-product companies, a shift in the sales mix from less profitable products to more profitable products will cause the company's break-even point to: a) increase; b) decrease; c) there will be no change in the break-even point; d) none of these.

___C___ 11. Herman Corp. has two products, A and B, with the following total sales and total variable costs:

	Product A	Product B
Sales	$10,000	$30,000
Variable expenses..........	$4,000	$24,000

What is the overall contribution margin ratio? a) 70%; b) 50%; c) 30%; d) 40%.

Exercises

6-1.   Hardee Company sells a single product. The selling price is $30 per unit and the variable expenses are $18 per unit. The company's most recent annual contribution format income statement is given below:

Sales..	$135,000
Less variable expenses........................	81,000
Contribution margin............................	54,000
Less fixed expenses	48,000
Net operating income..........................	$ 6,000

a.   Compute the contribution margin per unit. $ __12__

b.   Compute the CM ratio. __40__ %

c.   Compute the break-even point in sales dollars. $ __1200000__

d.   Compute the break-even point in units sold. __4000__ units

CM R: $\frac{CM}{Sales}$

60% : $\frac{CM}{200000}$

CM: 200000 × 60%
 = 1200

e.   How many units must be sold next year to double the company's profits? _5000_ units

f.   Compute the company's degree of operating leverage. _9_

g.   Sales for next year (in units) are expected to increase by 5%. Using the degree of operating leverage, compute the expected percentage increase in net operating income. _45_ %

h.   Verify your answer to part g above by preparing a contribution format income statement showing a 5% increase in sales.

Sales	$ 141750
Less variable expenses	85050
Contribution margin	56700
Less fixed expenses	48000
Net operating income	$ 8700

6-2.   Using the data below, construct a cost-volume-profit graph like the one in Exhibit 6-2 in the text:

Selling price: $10 per unit.
Variable expenses: $6 per unit.
Fixed expenses: $40,000 total.

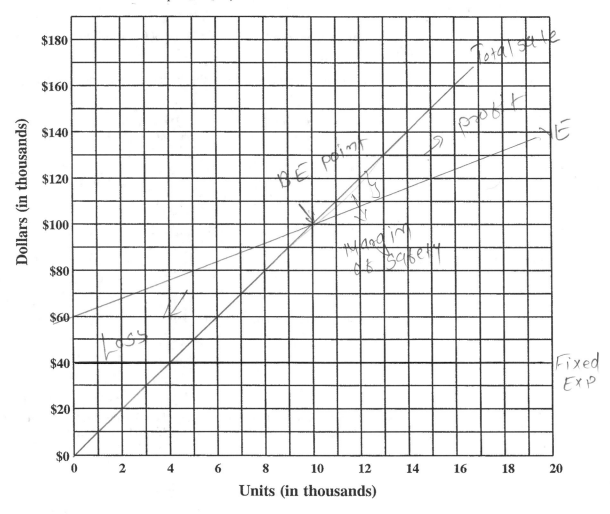

What is the break-even point in units? _____10,000_____.

What is the break-even point in total sales dollars? _____100000_____

65

6-3.   Seaver Company produces and sells two products, X and Y. Data concerning the products follow:

	Product X	*Product Y*
Selling price per unit	$10	$12
Variable expenses per unit......................	6	3
Contribution margin per unit	$ 4	$ 9

In the most recent month, the company sold 400 units of Product X and 600 units of Product Y. Fixed expenses are $5,000 per month.

a.   Complete the following contribution format income statement for the most recent month (carry percentages to one decimal point):

	Product X Amount	%	Product Y Amount	%	Total Amount	%
Sales...	$ 4000		$ 7200		$11200	
Less variable expenses.................	2400		1800		4200	
Contribution margin	$ 1600		$ 5400		7000	
Less fixed expenses					5000	
Net operating income (loss).........					$ 2000	

b.   Compute the company's overall monthly break-even point in sales dollars. $ _____

c.   If the company continues to sell 1,000 units, in total, each month, but the sales mix shifts so that an equal number of units of each product is being sold, would you expect monthly net operating income to rise or fall? Explain.

_____

_____

_____

_____

_____

d. Refer to the data in part c above. If the sales mix shifts as explained, would you expect the company's monthly break-even point to rise or fall? Explain.

_____

_____

_____

_____

_____

_____

Answers to Questions and Exercises

True or False

1. F The CM ratio is the unit contribution margin divided by the unit selling price. One product might have a higher unit contribution than another, but its selling price may be lower.

2. F The break-even point occurs where profit is zero and the contribution margin is equal to fixed expenses.

3. T The break-even point can be computed in terms of units sold or sales dollars.

4. T A change in sales mix usually results in a change in the overall CM ratio. If the overall CM ratio changes, the break-even point will also change.

5. T The CM ratio measures how much of a sales dollar is translated into increased contribution margin and profit.

6. F Profits should increase by $32\% = 4 \times 8\%$.

7. F The degree of operating leverage decreases as a company moves further and further from its break-even point.

8. T At the break-even point all fixed costs have been covered. All contribution margin generated from that point forward increases net operating income.

9. F The reverse is true—the overall break-even point will rise since the average CM ratio will be lower as a result of selling less profitable products.

10. T By definition, incremental analysis deals only with differences between alternatives.

11. F The reverse is true—one would expect the company's CM ratio to rise. Variable costs would be lower and hence the CM ratio would be higher.

12. F The break-even point is computed by dividing total *fixed costs* by the CM ratio.

13. T This is a key assumption since a change in the sales mix will change the break-even point.

Multiple Choice

1. c
Unit selling price	$50
Less unit variable expenses	30
Unit contribution margin	$20

2. b
Unit contribution margin	$ 20
Unit selling price	÷ $ 50
Contribution margin ratio	0.40

3. a

$$\frac{\text{Breakeven point}}{\text{in total sales dollars}} = \frac{\text{Fixed expenses}}{\text{CM ratio}}$$

$$= \frac{\$200,000}{0.40} = \$500,000$$

4. b

$$\frac{\text{Units sold}}{\text{to attain}} = \frac{\text{Fixed expenses} + \text{Target profit}}{\text{Unit contribution margin}}$$

$$= \frac{\$200,000 + \$50,000}{\$20} = 12,500 \text{ units}$$

5. c

$$\frac{\$90,000}{0.60} = \$150,000 \text{ break-even sales}$$

Margin of safety $= \$200,000 - \$150,000 = \$50,000$

6. d $\$50,000 \div \$200,000 = 25\%$

7. b
Sales	$200,000
CM ratio	× 0.60
Contribution margin	$120,000

8. d
Contribution margin	$120,000
Net operating income	÷ $30,000
Operating leverage	4.0

9. b The computations are:

$$\frac{\text{Percentage}}{\text{change in sales}} = \frac{\$450,000 - \$400,000}{\$400,000} = 12.5\%$$

Percentage change in dollar sales	12.5%
Degree of operating leverage	× 6.0
Percentage change in net operating income	75.0%

10. b A shift to more profitable products would result in an increase in the overall CM ratio. Thus, fewer sales would be needed to cover the fixed costs and the break-even point would therefore decrease.

11. c

	Product A	*Product B*	*Total*
Sales	$10,000	$30,000	$40,000
Variable expenses........	4,000	24,000	28,000
Contribution margin	$ 6,000	$ 6,000	$12,000

Overall CM ratio = $12,000 ÷ $40,000 = 30%

Exercises

6-1. a.

	Per Unit	
Selling price	$30	100%
Less variable expenses	18	60
Unit contribution margin	$12	40%

b. $\text{CM ratio} = \dfrac{\text{Contribution margin}}{\text{Sales}} = \dfrac{\$54,000}{\$135,000} = 40\%$

c. Sales = Variable expenses + Fixed expenses + Profits
$X = 0.60X + \$48,000 + \$0$
$0.40X = \$48,000$
$X = \$48,000 \div 0.40$
$X = \$120,000$

Alternative solution:

$\dfrac{\text{Breakeven point}}{\text{in total sales dollars}} = \dfrac{\text{Fixed expenses}}{\text{CM ratio}} = \dfrac{\$48,000}{0.40} = \$120,000$

d. Sales = Variable expenses + Fixed expenses + Profits
$\$30Q = \$18Q + \$48,000 + \$0$
$\$12Q = \$48,000$
$Q = \$48,000 \div \$12 \text{ per unit}$
$Q = 4,000 \text{ units}$

Alternative solution:

$\dfrac{\text{Breakeven point}}{\text{in units sold}} = \dfrac{\text{Fixed expenses}}{\text{Unit contribution margin}} = \dfrac{\$48,000}{\$12 \text{ per unit}} = 4,000 \text{ units}$

e. Sales = Variable expenses + Fixed expenses + Profits
$\$30Q = \$18Q + \$48,000 + \$12,000$
$\$12Q = \$60,000$
$Q = \$60,000 \div \$12 \text{ per unit}$
$Q = 5,000 \text{ units}$

Alternative solution:

$\dfrac{\text{Units sold to}}{\text{attain target profit}} = \dfrac{\text{Fixed expenses} + \text{Target profit}}{\text{Unit contribution margin}} = \dfrac{\$46,000 + \$12,000}{\$12 \text{ per unit}} = 5,000 \text{ units}$

f. $\dfrac{\text{Degree of operating}}{\text{leverage}} = \dfrac{\text{Contribution margin}}{\text{Net income}} = \dfrac{\$54,000}{\$6,000} = 9.0$

g.

Percentage change in dollar sales..................	5%
Degree of operating leverage	× 9.0
Percentage change in net operating income ..	45%

h. New sales volume: 4,500 units × 105% = 4,725 units

Sales (4,725 units @ $30 per unit)	$141,750
Less variable expenses (4,725 units @ $18 per unit)..	85,050
Contribution margin..	56,700
Less fixed expenses..	48,000
Net operating income	$ 8,700

Present net operating income	$ 6,000
Expected increase: $6,000 × 45%	2,700
Expected net operating income (as above).................	$ 8,700

6-2. The completed CVP graph:

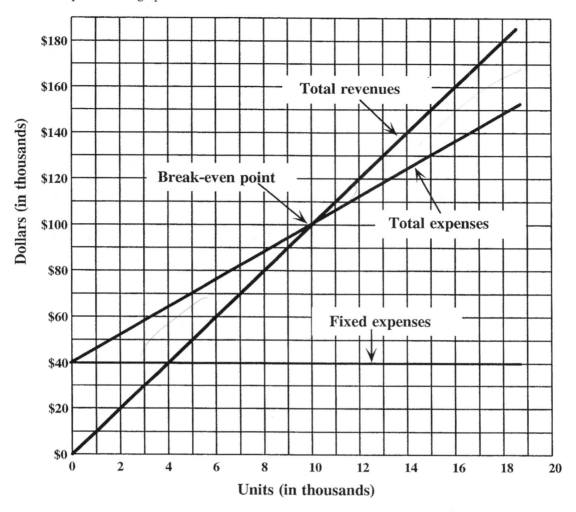

The break-even point is 10,000 units or $100,000 in dollar sales.

6-3.   a.   The completed income statement:

	Product X		Product Y		Total	
	Amount	*%*	*Amount*	*%*	*Amount*	*%*
Sales	$4,000	100	$7,200	100	$11,200	100.0
Less variable expenses	2,400	60	1,800	25	4,200	37.5
Contribution margin	$1,600	40	$5,400	75	7,000	62.5
Less fixed expenses................					5,000	
Net operating income					$ 2,000	

b. $$\frac{\text{Breakeven point}}{\text{in total sales dollars}} = \frac{\text{Fixed expenses}}{\text{CM ratio}} = \frac{\$5,000}{0.625} = \$8,000$$

c.   Monthly net operating income will fall. The shift in sales mix will mean that less of Product Y is being sold and more of Product X is being sold. Since Product Y has a higher contribution margin per unit than Product X, this means that less contribution margin in *total* will be available, and profits will therefore fall.

d.   The monthly break-even point will rise. As explained above, the shift in sales mix will be toward the less profitable Product X, which has a CM ratio of only 40% as compared to 75% for Product Y. Thus, the company's *overall* CM ratio will fall, and the break-even point will rise since less contribution margin will be available per unit to cover the fixed costs.

Chapter 7

Profit Planning

Chapter Study Suggestions

Carefully study Exhibit 7-2, which provides an overview of the budgeting process. Notice particularly how nearly all budgets eventually have an effect on the cash budget. As suggested by this exhibit, the cash budget is a key budget ties together much of the budgeting process. Schedule 8 in the text contains an example of a cash budget.

Schedules 1 and 2, containing the sales and production budgets, are also very important and your homework assignments are very likely to concentrate on these two budgets. As you proceed through the chapter, you will see that all other budgets depend in some way on the sales budget in Schedule 1. Notice that a schedule of expected cash collections accompanies the sales budget. Make sure you understand how the production budget is put together based on the sales budget and desired inventory levels.

CHAPTER HIGHLIGHTS

A. Profit planning is accomplished in most organizations with budgets. A *budget* is a detailed plan for the acquisition and use of financial and other resources over a specified time period.

    1. The master budget is a summary of the company's plans and goals for the future. It sets specific targets for sales, production, and financing activities and indicates the resources that will be supplied to meet those targets. The master budget culminates with a cash budget and a projected income statement and projected balance sheet.

    2. The budgeting process has two major aspects—planning and control.

        a. *Planning* involves developing objectives and formulating steps to achieve these objectives.

        b. *Control* involves the steps taken by management to increase the likelihood that the objectives set down at the planning stage are attained.

    3. Budgeting provides a number of benefits:

        a   The budget *communicates* management's plans throughout the entire organization.

        b. The budgeting process forces managers to *think ahead* and to *formalize* their planning efforts.

        c. The budgeting process provides a means of *allocating resources* to those parts of the organization where they can be used most effectively.

        d. Budgeting uncovers potential *bottlenecks* before they occur.

        e. The budget *coordinates* the activities of the entire organization by *integrating* the plans and objectives of the various parts.

        f. The budget provides goals and objectives that serve as *benchmarks* for evaluating subsequent performance.

B. This chapter and the next three chapters are concerned with *responsibility accounting*. The basic idea behind responsibility accounting is that each manager's performance should be judged by how well he or she manages those items—and only those items—under his or her control. Each manager is assigned responsibility for those items of revenues and costs in the budget that the manager is able to control to a significant extent. The manager is then held responsible for deviations between budgeted goals and actual results.

C. Budget preparation is a complex task requiring the cooperative effort of many managers.

    1. Operating budgets (the budgets discussed in this chapter) ordinarily cover a one-year period divided into quarters and months.

    2. Rather than imposing budgets from above or from the accounting department, managers should be involved in setting their own budgets . There are two reasons for this. First, managers are likely to have the best information concerning their own operations. Second, a manager who takes an active role in developing his or her own budget is more likely to be committed to attaining the budget.

D. The *master budget* consists of a number of separate but interdependent budgets. Exhibit 7-2 provides an overview of the master budget and shows how the parts of the master budget are linked together. Study this exhibit carefully.

    1. The *sales budget* (Schedule 1 in the text) is the beginning point in the budgeting process. It details the expected sales, in both units and dollars, for the budget period. The sales budget is accompanied by a *Schedule of Expected Cash Collections*, which shows the anticipated cash inflow from sales and collections of accounts receivable for the budget period.

    2. In a manufacturing company, the sales budget is followed by the *production budget* (Schedule 2 in the text), which shows what must be produced to meet sales forecasts and to provide for desired levels of inventory.

        a. The production budget has the following format:

Budgeted unit sales	XXX
Add desired ending inventory	XXX
Total needs	XXX
Less beginning inventory	XXX
Required production	XXX

        b. Study Schedule 2 in the text carefully. Note that the Year column is not simply the sum of the figures for the quarters in Schedule 2. The desired ending inventory for the year is the desired ending inventory for the 4th Quarter. And the beginning inventory for the year is the beginning inventory for the 1st Quarter. Warning: Students often overlook this important detail.

    3. In a merchandising company such as a clothing store, the sales budget is followed by a *merchandise purchases budget* instead of a production budget. This budget details the amount of goods that must be purchased from suppliers to meet customer demand and to maintain adequate stocks of ending inventory.

a. The format for the merchandise purchases budget is (in units or dollars):

Budgeted cost of goods sold............................ XXX
Add desired ending inventory XXX
Total needs XXX
Less beginning inventory XXX
Required purchases XXX

b. Note the similarity between the production budget in a manufacturing company and the merchandise purchases budget in a merchandising company.

4. In a manufacturing company, the *direct materials budget* follows the production budget. It details the amount of raw materials that must be acquired to support production and to provide for adequate inventories.

a. The format for the direct materials budget is:

Raw materials required for production............ XXX
Add desired ending inventory XXX
Total raw materials needs................................ XXX
Less beginning inventory XXX
Raw materials to be purchased........................ XXX

b. The direct materials budget should be accompanied by a *Schedule of Expected Cash Disbursements* for materials.

c. An example of a direct materials budget appears in Schedule 3 in the text. Note that the Year column is not simply the sum of the figures for the quarters.

5. In a manufacturing company, a *direct labor budget* (Schedule 4 in the text) also follows the production budget.

6. In a manufacturing company, a *manufacturing overhead budget* (Schedule 5 in the text) also follows the production budget and details all of the production costs that will be required other than direct materials and direct labor.

7. In a manufacturing company, the *ending finished goods inventory budget* (Schedule 6 in the text) provides computations of unit product costs and of the carrying value of the ending inventory.

8. In all types of companies, a *selling and administrative expense* budget (Schedule 7 in the text) is prepared.

9. The *cash budget* (Schedule 8 in the text) summarizes all of the cash inflows and cash outflows appearing on the various budgets. In many companies the cash budget is the single most important result of the budgeting process because it can provide critical advance warnings of potential cash problems. The cash budget allows managers to arrange for financing *before* a crisis develops. Potential lenders are more likely to provide financing if managers appear to be in control and looking ahead rather than simply reacting to crises.

a. The cash budget has the following format:

Cash balance, beginning................................... XXX
Add receipts.. XXX
Total cash available before current financing.. XXX
Less disbursements... XXX
Excess (deficiency) of cash available
   over disbursements XXX
Financing.. XXX
Cash balance, ending...................................... XXX

b. Study Schedule 8 with care, noting particularly how the financing section is handled.

c. As with the production budget and the direct materials budget, the Year column in Schedule 8 is not simply the sum of the figures for the quarters. The beginning cash balance for the year is the beginning cash balance for the 1st Quarter. And the ending cash balance for the year is the ending cash balance for the 4th Quarter.

10. The budgeting process culminates with the preparation of a *budgeted income statement* (Schedule 9 in the text) and a *budgeted balance sheet* (Schedule 10 in the text.)

REVIEW AND SELF-TEST
Questions and Exercises

True or False

Enter a T or an F in the blank to indicate whether the statement is true or false.

__T__ 1. The usual starting point in budgeting is to forecast sales.

__F__ 2. A self-imposed budget is one prepared by top management and imposed on other management levels as it is passed downward through an organization.

__F__ 3. Budgets are planning devices rather than control devices.

__T__ 4. The basic idea behind responsibility accounting is that each manager's performance should be judged by how well he or she manages those items under his or her control.

__F__ 5. Ending inventories occur because an organization is unable to sell all that it had planned to sell during a period.

__F__ 6. The required production in units for a budget period is equal to the expected unit sales for the period.

__F__ 7. Because of the technical nature of budgeting, it is best to leave budgeting entirely in the capable hands of the accounting staff.

Multiple Choice

Choose the best answer or response by placing the identifying letter in the space provided.

__a__ 1. Actual sales in Ward Company were $30,000 in June, $50,000 in July, and $70,000 in August. Budgeted sales in September are $60,000. Thirty percent of a month's sales are collected in the month of sale, 50% in the first month after sale, 15% in the second month after sale, and the remaining 5% are uncollectible. Budgeted cash receipts for September should be: a) $60,500; b) $62,000; c) $57,000; d) $70,000.

__c__ 2. Beecher Inc. is planning to purchase inventory for resale costing $90,000 in October, $70,000 in November, and $40,000 in December. The company pays for 40% of its purchases in the month of purchase and 60% in the month following purchase. What would be the budgeted cash disbursements for purchases of inventory in December? a) $40,000; b) $70,000; c) $58,000; d) $200,000.

__b__ 3. Archer Company has budgeted sales of 30,000 units in April, 40,000 units in May, and 60,000 units in June. The company has 6,000 units on hand on April 1. If the company requires an ending inventory equal to 20% of the following month's sales, production during May should be: a) 32,000 units; b) 44,000 units; c) 36,000 units; d) 40,000 units.

__a__ 4. Refer to the data for Archer Company in question 3. Each unit requires 3 pounds of a material. A total of 24,000 pounds of the material were on hand on April 1, and the company requires materials on hand at the end of each month equal to 25% of the following month's production needs. The company plans to produce 32,000 units of finished goods in April. How many pounds of the material should the company plan to purchase in April? a) 105,000; b) 19,000; c) 87,000; d) 6,000.

__a__ 5. If the beginning cash balance is $15,000, the required ending cash balance is $12,000, cash disbursements are $125,000, and cash collections from customers are $90,000, the company must borrow: a) $32,000; b) $20,000; c) $8,000; d) $38,000.

Exercises

7-1.   Billings Company produces and sells a single product. Budgeted sales for the next four months are given below:

	April	May	June	July
Budgeted unit sales	10,000	12,000	15,000	9,000

The company needs a production budget for the second quarter. Experience indicates that end-of-month inventories should equal 10% of the following month's sales in units. At the end of March, 1,000 units were on hand. Complete the following production budget for the quarter:

	April	May	June	Quarter
Budgeted sales..	10,000	12000	15000	37000
Add desired ending inventory	1200	1500	900	900
Total needs	11200	13500	15900	37900
Less beginning inventory	1000	1200	1500	1000
Required production......................................	10200	12300	14400	36900

7-2.   Dodero Company's production budget for the next four months is given below:

	July	August	September	October
Required production..................	15,000	18,000	20,000	16,000

Each unit of product uses five ounces of raw materials. At the end of June, 11,250 ounces of material were on hand. The company wants to maintain an inventory of materials equal to 15% of the following month's production needs.

Complete the following materials purchases budget for the third quarter:

	July	August	September	Quarter
Required production (units)	15000	18000	20000	53000
Raw material needed per unit (ounces)	5	5	5	5
Production needs (ounces)	75000	90000	100000	265000
Add desired ending inventory (ounces)..............	13500	15000	12000	12000
Total needs (ounces)	88500	105000	112000	277000
Less beginning inventory (ounces).....................	11250	13500	15000	11250
Raw materials to be purchased (ounces)	77250	91500	97000	265750

7-3.   Whitefish Company budgets its cash two months at a time. Budgeted cash disbursements for March and April, respectively, are: for inventory purchases, $90,000 and $82,000; for selling and administrative expenses (includes $5,000 depreciation each month), $75,000 and $70,000; for equipment purchases, $15,000 and $6,000; and for dividend payments, $5,000 and $0. Budgeted cash collections from customers are $150,000 and $185,000 for March and April, respectively. The company will begin March with a $10,000 cash balance on hand. There should be a minimum cash balance of $5,000 at the end of each month. If needed, the company can borrow money at 12% per year. All borrowings are at the beginning of a month, and all repayments are at the end of a month. Interest is paid only when principal is repaid.

Complete the following cash budget for March and April:

	March	April	Two Months
Cash balance, beginning..	10,000	5000	
Add collections from customers.............................	150000	185000	
Total cash available...	160000	190000	
Less disbursements:			
Inv. Purchase 90.000	90,000	82000	
Selling & admi 70,000	70,000	65000	
Equip pur. 15.000	15000	6000	
divi 5000	5000	0	
Total disbursements	180000	153000	
Excess (deficiency) of cash available over disbursements	−20,000	37000	
Financing:			
Borrowings (at beginning).....................................	25000		
Repayments (at ending)		25000	
Interest (12% per year)		500	
Total financing	25000	25500	
Cash balance, ending..	5000	11500	

Answers to Questions and Exercises

True or False

1. T   A sales forecast is the basis for the company's sales budget. The sales budget, in turn, is the basis for most of the other parts of the master budget.

2. F   A self-imposed budget is one in which a manager prepares his or her own budget estimates.

3. F   Budgeting involves both planning and control. Once a budget is set, it then becomes a control device. It is the benchmark for assessing actual results.

4. T   This is a clear, straightforward statement of the purpose of responsibility accounting.

5. F   Ending inventories are carefully planned if a company is following good budget procedures.

6. F   Production requirements are determined by the level of beginning inventory and the desired level of ending inventory as well as by the expected unit sales.

7. F   The accounting staff may provide help in preparing budgets, but the underlying estimates and data must come from operating managers. There are two reasons for this. First, the operating managers generally have better information about their own operations than the accounting staff. Second, the operating managers must be involved in preparing their own budgets or they will not be committed to them.

Multiple Choice

1. a   The computations are:

September sales, ($60,000 × 30%)	$18,000
August sales, ($70,000 × 50%)	35,000
July sales, ($50,000 × 15%)	7,500
Total cash receipts	$60,500

2. c   The computations are:

November purchases ($70,000 × 60%)	$42,000
December purchases ($40,000 × 40%)	16,000
Total cash disbursements	$58,000

3. b   The computations are:

Budgeted sales	40,000
Desired ending inventory (20% × 60,000)	12,000
Total needs	52,000
Less beginning inventory (20% × 40,000)	8,000
Required production	44,000

4. a   The computations are:

Required production	32,000
Material per unit	× 3 lbs
Production needs	96,000
Desired ending inventory (25% × 44,000 × 3 lbs)	33,000
Total needs	129,000
Less beginning inventory (25% × 96,000 lbs)	24,000
Required purchases	105,000

5. a   The computations are:

Beginning cash balance	$ 15,000
Cash receipts	90,000
Cash available	105,000
Cash disbursements	125,000
Deficiency of cash	$(20,000)

Since the company desires an ending cash balance of $12,000, the company must borrow $32,000 to make up for the cash deficiency of $20,000.

Exercises

7-1.

	April	May	June	Quarter
Budgeted unit sales	10,000	12,000	15,000	37,000
Add desired ending inventory	1,200	1,500	900	900
Total needs	11,200	13,500	15,900	37,900
Less beginning inventory	1,000	1,200	1,500	1,000
Required production	10,200	12,300	14,400	36,900

7-2.

	July	August	September	Quarter
Required production (units)	15,000	18,000	20,000	53,000
Raw material needs per unit (ounces)	× 5 oz	× 5 oz	× 5 oz	× 5 oz
Production needs (ounces)	75,000	90,000	100,000	265,000
Add desired ending inventory (ounces)	13,500	15,000	12,000*	12,000
Total needs (ounces)	88,500	105,000	112,000	277,000
Less beginning inventory (ounces)	11,250	13,500	15,000	11,250
Raw materials to be purchased (ounces)	77,250	91,500	97,000	265,750

*16,000 units for October × 5 oz = 80,000 oz; 80,000 oz × 15% = 12,000 oz

7-3.

	March	April	Two Months
Cash balance, beginning	$ 10,000	$ 5,000	$ 10,000
Add collections from customers	150,000	185,000	335,000
Total cash available	160,000	190,000	345,000
Less disbursements:			
Inventory purchases	90,000	82,000	172,000
Selling and administrative expenses (net of depreciation)	70,000	65,000	135,000
Equipment purchases	15,000	6,000	21,000
Dividends	5,000	—	5,000
Total disbursements	180,000	153,000	333,000
Excess (deficiency) of cash available over cash disbursements	(20,000)	37,000	12,000
Financing:			
Borrowings (at beginning)	25,000		25,000
Repayments (at ending)		(25,000)	(25,000)
Interest (12% per year)		(500)*	(500)
Total financing	25,000	(25,500)	(500)
Cash balance, ending	$ 5,000	$ 11,500	$11,500

* $25,000 × 12% × 2/12 = $500

Chapter 8

Standard Costs

Chapter Study Suggestions

The first part of the chapter covers setting standard costs. Exhibit 8-2 presents a standard cost card, which is the final product of the standard setting process. The second part of the chapter covers standard cost variance analysis. Exhibit 8-3 provides an overall perspective of variance analysis. Exhibits 8-4 through 8-7 give detailed examples of the analysis of materials, labor, and variable overhead. Notice that the data from the standard cost card in Exhibit 8-2 are used in Exhibits 8-4, 8-5, and 8-6. As you study, follow the data from Exhibit 8-2 into the following exhibits. This will help you tie the various parts of the chapter together into one integrated whole.

CHAPTER HIGHLIGHTS

A. A *standard* is a benchmark for evaluating performance. Manufacturing companies commonly set standards for materials, labor, and overhead for each product. Some service companies, such as auto repair shops and fast food outlets also set standards.

1. Standards are set for both the quantity and the price (cost) of inputs.

2. Actual quantities and prices of inputs are compared to the standards. Differences are called variances. Only the significant variances are brought to the attention of management. This is called *management by exception.*

B. Setting accurate quantity and price standards is a vital step in the control process.

1. Many persons should be involved in setting standards: accountants, purchasing agents, industrial engineers, production supervisors, and line managers.

2. Standards tend to fall into two categories—either ideal or practical.

a. Ideal standards can be attained only by working at top efficiency 100% of the time. They allow for no machine breakdowns or lost time.

b. Practical standards, by contrast, allow for breakdowns and normal lost time (such as for rest breaks). Practical standards are standards that are "tight, but attainable."

c. Most managers feel that practical standards provide better motivation than ideal standards. The use of ideal standards can easily lead to frustration.

3. Direct material standards are set for both the price and the quantity of the material inputs that go into units of product.

a. Price standards should reflect the final, delivered cost of materials. This price should include freight, handling, and other costs necessary to get the material into a condition ready to use. It should also reflect any cash discounts allowed.

b. Quantity standards should reflect the amount of material that is required to make one unit of product, including allowances for unavoidable waste, spoilage, and other normal inefficiencies.

4. Direct labor price and quantity standards are expressed in terms of the labor rate and labor hours.

a. The standard direct labor rate per hour should include not only wages but also fringe benefits, employment taxes, and other labor related costs.

b. The standard labor-hours per unit should include allowances for rest breaks, personal needs of employees, cleanup, and machine down time.

5. As with direct labor, the price and quantity standards for variable overhead are generally expressed in terms of a rate and hours. The rate represents the variable portion of the predetermined overhead rate. The quantity is usually expressed in terms of direct labor-hours or machine-hours.

6. The price and quantity standards for materials, labor, and overhead are summarized on the *standard cost card*. Essentially, the standard cost per unit represents the budgeted variable production cost for a single unit of product.

C. The General Variance Model. A *variance* is a difference between standard prices and actual prices or standard quantities and actual quantities. The general model in Exhibit 8-3 is very helpful in variance analysis. Study this model with care.

1. A price variance and a quantity variance can be computed for each of the three variable cost categories—materials, labor, and overhead.

2. The *standard quantity allowed for the output* is the amount of an input that *should have been used* to complete the output of the period. This is a key concept in the chapter!

D. Direct Materials Variances. Exhibit 8-4 illustrates the variance analysis of direct materials. As you study the exhibit, notice that the center column (Actual Quantity of Inputs, at Standard Price) plays a part in the computation of both the price and quantity variances.

1. The *materials price variance* can be expressed in formula form as:

$$\text{Price variance} = (AQ \times AP) - (AQ \times SP)$$
or
$$\text{Price variance} = AQ (AP - SP)$$

where:
AQ = Actual quantity of inputs purchased
AP = Actual price of inputs purchased
SP = Standard price of inputs

An unfavorable materials price variance has many possible causes including high purchase prices, excessive freight costs, failure to take advantage of quantity discounts, improper grade of materials purchased, rush orders, and inaccurate standards.

2. The *materials quantity variance* can be expressed in formula form as:

$$\text{Quantity variance} = (AQ \times SP) - (SQ \times SP)$$
or
$$\text{Quantity variance} = SP\,(AQ - SQ)$$

where:
AQ = Actual quantity of inputs used
SQ = Standard quantity of input allowed
      for the actual output
SP = Standard price of inputs

Possible causes of an unfavorable materials quantity variance include untrained workers, faulty machines, low quality materials, and inaccurate standards.

3. The materials price variance is usually computed when materials are purchased, whereas the materials quantity variance is computed when materials are used in production. Consequently, the price variance is computed based on the amount of material purchased whereas the quantity variance is computed based on the amount of material used in production.

E. Direct Labor Variances. Exhibit 8-6 shows the variance analysis of direct labor. Notice that the format is the same as for direct materials, but the terms "rate" and "hours" are used in place of the terms "price" and "quantity".

1. The price variance for labor is called the *labor rate variance*. The formula is:

$$\text{Rate variance} = (AH \times AR) - (AH \times SR)$$
or
$$\text{Rate variance} = AH\,(AR - SR)$$

where:
AH = Actual labor hours
AR = Actual labor wage rate
SR = Standard labor wage rate

Possible causes of an unfavorable labor rate variance include poor assignment of workers to jobs, unplanned overtime, pay increases, and inaccurate standards.

2. The quantity variance for labor is called the *labor efficiency variance*. The formula is:

$$\text{Efficiency variance} = (AH \times SR) - (SH \times SR)$$
or
$$\text{Efficiency variance} = SR\,(AH - SH)$$

where:
AH = Actual labor hours
SH = Standard labor hours allowed
      for the actual output
SR = Standard labor wage rate

Possible causes of an unfavorable labor efficiency variance include poorly trained workers, low quality materials, faulty equipment, poor supervision, insufficient work to keep everyone busy, and inaccurate standards.

F. Variable Manufacturing Overhead Variances. Exhibit 8-7 illustrates the variance analysis of variable manufacturing overhead. Notice that the format is the same as for direct labor.

1. The price or rate variance for variable manufacturing overhead is called the *variable overhead spending variance*. The formula for this variance is:

$$\text{Spending variance} = (AH \times AR) - (AH \times SR)$$
or
$$\text{Spending variance} = AH\,(AR - SR)$$

where:
AH = Actual hours (usually labor hours)
AR = Actual variable manufacturing
      overhead rate
SR = Standard variable manufacturing
      overhead rate

2. The quantity, or efficiency, variance for variable manufacturing overhead is called the *variable overhead efficiency variance*. The formula for this variance is:

$$\text{Efficiency variance} = (AH \times SR) - (SH \times SR)$$
or
$$\text{Efficiency variance} = SR\,(AH - SH)$$

where:
AH = Actual hours (usually labor hours)
SH = Standard hours allowed for
      the actual output
SR = Standard variable manufacturing
      overhead rate

G. Not all differences between standard costs and quantities and actual costs and quantities warrant management attention. The manager should focus on the differences that are significant.

H. There are some potential problems with the use of standard costs. Most of these problems result from improper use of standard costs and the management by exception principle or from using standard costs in situations in which they are not appropriate.

1. Standard cost variance reports are usually prepared on a monthly basis and may be released too late to be really useful. Some companies are now reporting variances and other key operating data daily or even more frequently.

2. Managers must avoid using variance reports as a way to find someone to blame. Management by ex-

ception, by its nature, tends to focus on the negative. Managers should remember to reward workers for a job well done.

3. If labor is fixed, the only way to avoid an unfavorable labor efficiency variance is to keep labor busy all the time producing output—even if there is no demand. This can lead to excess work in process and finished goods inventories.

4. A favorable variance may not be good. For example, Pizza Haven has a standard for the amount of mozzarella cheese on a 9-inch pizza. A favorable materials quantity variance means that less cheese was used than the standard specifies. The result is a substandard pizza.

5. There can be a tendency with standard cost reporting systems to emphasize meeting the standards to the exclusion of other important objectives such as maintaining and improving quality, on-time delivery, and customer satisfaction.

6. Just meeting standards may not be sufficient; continual improvement may be necessary.

Appendix 8A: General Ledger Entries to Record Variances

A. Many companies carry inventories at standard cost and record standard cost variances in the general ledger. This simplifies bookkeeping.

B. Favorable variances are recorded as credits, and unfavorable variances are recorded as debits.

1. The entry to record an unfavorable material price variance upon purchase of materials on account would be:

Raw Materials	XXX	
Materials Price Variance (U)	XXX	
Accounts Payable		XXX

2. The entry to record a favorable material quantity variance would be:

Work in Process	XXX	
Materials Quantity Variance (F)		XXX
Raw Materials		XXX

3. The entry to record an unfavorable labor efficiency variance and a favorable labor rate variance would be:

Work in Process	XXX	
Labor Efficiency Variance (U)	XXX	
Labor Rate Variance (F)		XXX
Wages Payable		XXX

REVIEW AND SELF-TEST
Questions and Exercises

True or False

Enter a T or an F in the blank to indicate whether the statement is true or false.

__T__ 1. Practical standards are generally viewed as better than ideal standards for motivating employees.

__F__ 2. Ideal standards allow for machine break-down time and other normal inefficiencies.

__F__ 3. In determining a material price standard, any freight or handling costs should be excluded.

__T__ 4. The standard rate for variable overhead consists of the variable portion of the predetermined overhead rate.

__F__ 5. Raw materials price variances should be computed and reported only when materials are placed into production.

__T__ 6. Variances similar to price and quantity variances can be computed for materials, labor, and overhead.

__F__ 7. Waste on the production line will result in a materials price variance.

__T__ 8. If the actual price or quantity exceeds the standard price or quantity, the variance is unfavorable.

__F__ 9. Labor rate variances are largely out of the control of management.

__F__ 10. Managers should thoroughly investigate all differences (variances) between standard cost and actual cost.

__T__ 11. In a company with fixed labor, an undue focus on labor efficiency variances may result in the production of needless inventories.

__T__ 12. (Appendix 8A) The use of standard costs simplifies bookkeeping.

__T__ 13. (Appendix 8A) An unfavorable variance would be recorded as a debit in the general ledger.

Multiple Choice

Choose the best answer or response by placing the identifying letter in the space provided.

__B__ 1. The labor rate variance is determined by multiplying the difference between the actual labor rate and the standard labor rate by: a) the standard hours allowed; b) the actual hours worked; c) the budgeted hours allowed; d) none of these.

____ 2. If inferior-grade materials are purchased, the result may be: a) an unfavorable materials price variance; b) a favorable materials price variance; c) an unfavorable labor efficiency variance; d) a favorable labor efficiency variance; e) responses b and c are both correct; f) responses a and d are both correct.

__a__ 3. During June, Bradley Company produced 4,000 units of product. The standard cost card indicates the following labor standards per unit of output: 3.5 hours at $6 per hour = $21. During the month, the company worked 15,000 hours. The standard hours allowed for the month were: a) 14,000 hours; b) 15,000 hours; c) 24,000 hours; d) 18,000 hours.

____ 4. Refer to the data in question 3 above. What is the labor efficiency variance for June? (F indicates a Favorable variance and U indicates an Unfavorable variance.) a) $1,000 F; b) $1,000 U; c) $6,000 F; d) $6,000 U.

____ 5. Refer to the data in question 3 above. The total labor cost during June was $88,000 for the 15,000 hours that were worked. What is the labor rate variance for June? a) $6,000 F; b) $6,000 U; c) $2,000 F; d) $2,000 U.

____ 6. During July, Bradley Company produced 3,000 units of product. The standard cost card indicates the following materials standards per unit of output: 2 pounds at $0.50 per pound = $1. During July, 8,000 pounds of material were purchased at a cost of $3,900. The materials price variance for July is: a) $100 F; b) $100 U; c) $4,100 F; d) $4,100 U.

____ 7. Refer to the data in question 6 above. 6,100 pounds of material were used in July to produce the output of 3,000 units. The materials quantity variance for July is: a) $1,550 F; b) $1,550 U; c) $50 F; d) $50 U.

___ 8. During August, Bradley, Inc. produced 3,500 units of product using 12,750 labor hours. The standard cost card indicates the following variable manufacturing overhead standards per unit of output: 3.5 labor-hours at $2 per labor-hour = $7. During the month, the actual variable manufacturing overhead cost incurred was $25,000. The variable overhead spending variance was: a) $500 U; b) $500 F; c) $24,500 U; d) $24,500 F.

___ 9. Refer to the data in question 8 above. The variable overhead efficiency variance was: a) $7,000 F; b) $7,000 U; c) $1,000 F; d) $1,000 U.

b 10. The "price" variance for variable overhead is called a: a) rate variance; b) spending variance; c) budget variance; d) none of these.

Exercises

8-1. Selected data relating to Miller Company's operations for April are given below:

Number of units produced .... 500 units
Number of actual direct labor-hours worked .... 1,400 hours
Total actual direct labor cost $10,850

The standard cost card indicates that 2.5 hours of direct labor time is allowed per unit, at a rate of $8 per hour.

a. Complete the following analysis of direct labor cost for the month:

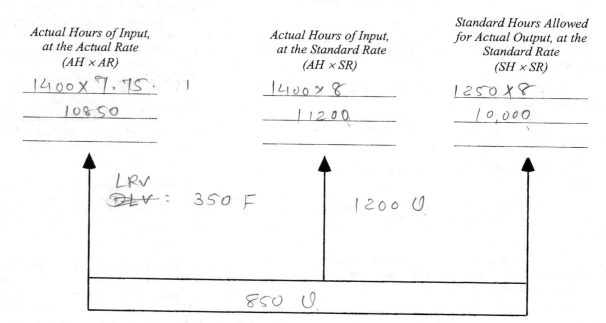

Actual Hours of Input, at the Actual Rate (AH × AR)	*Actual Hours of Input, at the Standard Rate (AH × SR)*	*Standard Hours Allowed for Actual Output, at the Standard Rate (SH × SR)*
1400 × 7.75	1400 × 8	1250 × 8
10850	11200	10,000

LRV
~~DLV~~ : 350 F   1200 U

850 U

b. Redo the above analysis of direct labor cost for the month, using the following formulas:

Labor Rate Variance = AH (AR – SR)
1400 (7.75 - 8)
= 1400 (0.25) = 350 F

Labor Efficiency Variance = SR (AH – SH)
8 (1400 - 1250)
= 8 (150)
= 1200 U

= 850 U.

8-2. The following activity took place in Solo Company during May:

Number of units produced .... 450 units
Material purchased .... 1,500 feet
Material used in production........................... 720 feet
Cost per foot for material purchased $3

The standard cost card indicates that 1.5 feet of materials are allowed for each unit of product. The standard cost of the materials is $4 per foot.

a. Complete the following analysis of direct materials cost for the month:

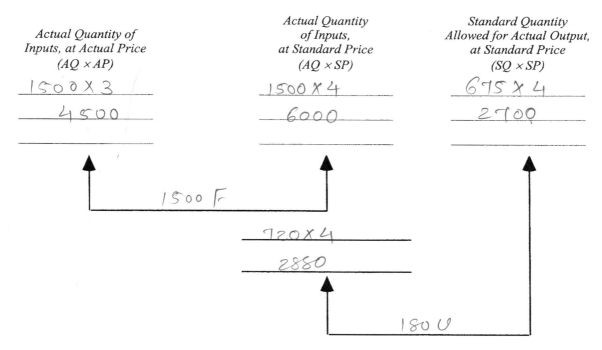

Actual Quantity of Inputs, at Actual Price $(AQ \times AP)$	*Actual Quantity of Inputs, at Standard Price* $(AQ \times SP)$	*Standard Quantity Allowed for Actual Output, at Standard Price* $(SQ \times SP)$
1500 X 3	1500 X 4	675 X 4
4500	6000	2700

1500 F

720 X 4
2880

180 U

(A total variance can't be computed in this situation, since the amount of materials purchased differs from the amount of materials used in production.)

b. Redo the above analysis of direct materials cost for the month, using the following formulas:

$$\text{Materials Price Variance} = AQ\,(AP - SP)$$

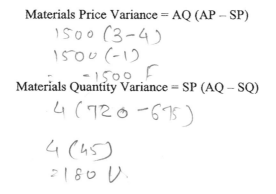

1500 (3−4)
1500 (−1)
= −1500 F

$$\text{Materials Quantity Variance} = SP\,(AQ - SQ)$$

4 (720 −675)

4 (45)
= 180 U.

8-3.   (Appendix 8A) Refer to the data for Solo Company in Exercise 8-2 on the previous page. Prepare journal entries to record all activity relating to direct materials for the month:

	Debit	Credit

Answers to Questions and Exercises

True or False

1. T Practical standards provide better motivation because they are attainable by workers.

2. F Ideal standards do not allow for either machine breakdowns or other normal inefficiencies.

3. F Freight and handling costs should be included in the material price standard since the purchasing manager should be responsible for the total cost of acquiring materials.

4. T This statement is true by definition.

5. F The purchasing manager is responsible for the materials price variance. This variance should be computed when the purchasing manager does his or her work—not when the materials are put into production.

6. T This point is illustrated in Exhibit 8-3.

7. F Waste will result in a materials quantity variance.

8. T This statement is true by definition.

9. F Labor rate variances can arise from how labor is used, and the use of labor is within the control of management.

10. F Managers should not waste time investigating insignificant variances.

11. T When labor is fixed, the only way to generate a more favorable labor efficiency variance is to keep everyone busy producing output—even if there is no demand.

12. T The use of standard costs simplifies the bookkeeping process since standards permit all units to be carried at the same cost.

13. T Unfavorable variances have the effect of decreasing income. Therefore, they are debit entries just as an expense is a debit entry.

Multiple Choice

1. b This point is illustrated in Exhibit 8-6.

2. e The materials price variance will probably be favorable, since the inferior grade materials probably will cost less. The labor efficiency variance will probably be unfavorable, since the inferior grade materials will probably require more work.

3. a The computation is: 4,000 units × 3.5 hours per unit = 14,000 standard hours.

4. d Efficiency variance = SR (AH − SH)
$$= \$6\,(15{,}000 - 14{,}000)$$
$$= \$6{,}000\ U$$

5. c Rate variance = (AH × AR) − (AH × SR)
$$= (\$88{,}000) - (15{,}000 \times \$6)$$
$$= \$2{,}000\ F$$

6. a Price variance = (AQ × AP) − (AQ × SP)
$$= (\$3{,}900) - (8{,}000 \times \$0.50)$$
$$= \$100\ F$$

7. d Quantity variance = SP (AQ − SQ)
$$= \$0.50\,(6{,}100 - 2 \times 3{,}000)$$
$$= \$50\ U$$

8. b Spending
variance = (AH × AR) − (AH × SR)
$$= (\$25{,}000) - (12{,}750 \times \$2)$$
$$= \$500\ F$$

9. d Efficiency variance = SR (AH − SH)
$$= \$2\,(12{,}750 - 3.5 \times 3{,}500)$$
$$= \$1{,}000\ U$$

10. b This point is illustrated in Exhibit 8-3.

Exercises

8-1.   a.

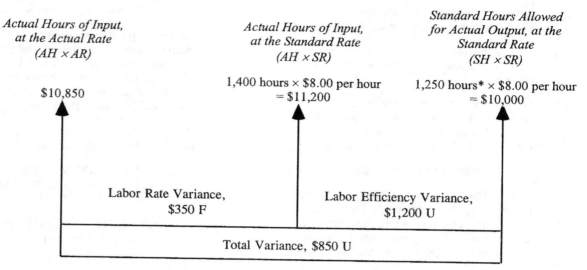

Actual Hours of Input, at the Actual Rate (AH × AR)	Actual Hours of Input, at the Standard Rate (AH × SR)	Standard Hours Allowed for Actual Output, at the Standard Rate (SH × SR)
$10,850	1,400 hours × $8.00 per hour = $11,200	1,250 hours* × $8.00 per hour = $10,000

Labor Rate Variance, $350 F

Labor Efficiency Variance, $1,200 U

Total Variance, $850 U

*500 units × 2.5 hours per unit = 1,250 hours

b.   AR = $10,850 ÷ 1,400 hours = $7.75 per hour
Labor Rate Variance = AH (AR − SR)
        = 1,400 hours ($7.75 per hour − $8.00 per hour) = $350 F

Labor Efficiency Variance = SR (AH − SH)
        = $8.00 per hour (1,400 hours − 1,250 hours) = $1,200 U

8-2.   a.

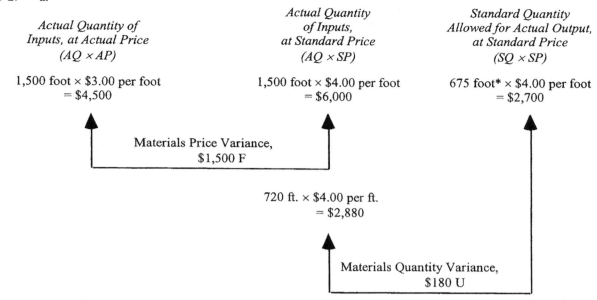

*450 units × 1.5 feet per unit = 675 feet

b.   Materials Price Variance = AQ (AP − SP)
              = 1,500 feet ($3.00 per foot − $4.00 per foot) = $1,500 F
      Materials Quantity Variance = SP (AQ − SQ)
              = $4.00 per foot (720 feet − 675 feet) = $180 U

Note that more materials were purchased (1,500 feet) than were used in production (720 feet). When computing the price variance, use the quantity of materials purchased. When computing the quantity variance, use the quantity of materials used in production.

8-3.

Raw Materials	6,000	
Materials Price Variance		1,500
Accounts Payable		4,500
Work in Process	2,700	
Materials Quantity Variance	180	
Raw Materials		2,880

Chapter 9

Flexible Budgets and Overhead Analysis

Chapter Study Suggestions

The chapter is divided into three parts. The first part covers flexible budgets, with Exhibit 9-3 providing a comprehensive example of how a flexible budget is prepared. Pay close attention to the differences between a flexible budget and a static budget.

The middle part of the chapter expands on the variance analysis of variable overhead that was introduced in Chapter 8. Exhibits 9-6 and 9-7 are the key exhibits here.

The last part of the chapter covers fixed overhead analysis. Three things in this part deserve special attention. First, understand what the "denominator activity" is, and how it is used. Second, be sure you understand the difference between a "normal-cost system" and a "standard-cost system," as illustrated in Exhibit 9-9. Third, be sure you understand the variance analysis of fixed overhead illustrated in Exhibit 9-10.

The chapter concludes with a detailed example of flexible budgets and fixed overhead analysis. Follow the example through step by step before attempting homework assignments.

CHAPTER HIGHLIGHTS

A. The sales budget, production budget, and cash budget in Chapter 7 are *static budgets.* They are static in the sense that they represent costs at a single level of activity. Since actual activity rarely coincides with the original activity level assumed in the static budget, a static budget should not be used to assess how well costs were controlled.. For example, if actual activity is higher than was assumed in the original, static budget, then variable costs should be higher than originally budgeted.

B. A *flexible budget* is geared to a range of activity, rather than to a single level. This can be seen from the flexible budget presented in Exhibit 9-3. Notice especially how a "cost formula" is used in the flexible budget for the variable costs.

1. The flexible budget is a dynamic tool. It can be used to quickly develop a budget for any level of activity within the relevant range. The variable costs are adjusted by multiplying the cost per unit by the activity level. Fixed costs remain unchanged within the relevant range.

2. The activity base underlying the flexible budget must be carefully chosen. Three general criteria are used in selecting an activity base:

    a. The flexible budget assumes that variable costs change in proportion to changes in the activity base, so the activity base should actually drive the variable costs.

    b. The activity base should not be expressed in dollars. For example, direct labor cost should not be used as an activity base. A change in the labor wage rate would change the measure of activity, but would have little real effect on variable costs such as the cost of supplies.

    c. The activity base should be simple and easy to understand.

C. A *flexible budget performance report* is used to evaluate how well costs were controlled.

1. Compute the amount for each variable cost in the flexible budget by multiplying its cost per unit by the actual level of activity for the period.

2. If the actual activity is within the relevant range, the fixed cost amounts are constant and can be copied from the static budget.

3. Variances are computed for each of the costs. If the actual cost exceeds the flexible budget cost for the actual level of activity, the variance is unfavorable. If the actual cost is less than the flexible budget cost

for the actual level of activity, the variance is favorable.

4. Actual fixed costs can differ from budgeted fixed costs and therefore fixed costs can have variances.

    a. A cost is fixed if it does not depend on the level of activity. However, a fixed cost can change for other reasons.

    b. For example, the cost of heating and lighting an administrative office is fixed—it does not depend on how many goods or services the company sells. Nevertheless, this cost can change from period to period due to seasonal factors, how conscientious people are in turning off lights, the thermostat setting, and so on.

    c. It is often easier to control fixed costs than variable costs. Many fixed costs involve discretionary activities such as travel costs, entertainment, and executive seminars.

D. The middle portion of the chapter focuses on variable manufacturing overhead. Two types of *variable overhead performance reports* are illustrated. One type of report shows just a spending variance. The other type of report shows both a spending and an efficiency variance. Both of these variances were discussed in Chapter 8.

1. If the flexible budget allowances in the performance report are based on the actual number of hours worked during the period, then there will be just a spending variance. Exhibit 9-6 illustrates this procedure. The overhead spending variance combines both price and quantity variances. An unfavorable variance could occur because the standard is in error, prices paid for overhead items were too high, or too many overhead resources were used.

2. If the flexible budget allowances in the performance report are based on both the actual number of hours worked and the standard hours allowed for the output of the period, both a spending and an efficiency variance can be computed.

    a. Exhibit 9-7 contains a performance report using this approach. Study the column headings in this exhibit carefully.

    b. The term "variable overhead efficiency variance" is a misnomer. This variance has nothing to do with how efficiently or inefficiently variable overhead resources were used. The inefficiency is really in the base underlying the application of overhead. For example, if direct labor-hours are used as the activity base, an unfavorable variable overhead efficiency variance will occur whenever the actual direct labor-hours exceeds the standard number of direct labor-hours allowed for the actual output.

E. The flexible budget can serve as the basis for computing predetermined overhead rates for product costing purposes. The formula is:

$$\text{Predetermined overhead rate} = \frac{\text{Overhead from the flexible budget for the denominator level of activity}}{\text{Denominator level of activity}}$$

1. The denominator level of activity is whatever level of activity that is assumed when the predetermined overhead rate is computed. The numerator in the rate is the amount of manufacturing overhead from the flexible budget for that level of activity.

2. The predetermined overhead rate can be divided into two parts, one for the variable overhead costs and the other for the fixed overhead costs. The fixed portion of the predetermined overhead rate depends on the level of the denominator activity that is chosen. The larger the denominator activity, the lower the rate will be.

F. Exhibit 9-9 is an extremely important exhibit. It shows that overhead is applied to work in process differently under a *standard cost system* than it is under a *normal cost system.*

1. We studied normal cost systems in Chapter 2. In a normal cost system, overhead is applied by multiplying the predetermined overhead rate by the actual hours of activity for a period.

2. In contrast, under a standard cost system overhead is applied to work in process by multiplying the predetermined overhead rate by the *standard hours allowed for the output of the period.* As in Chapter 8, the standard hours allowed for the output are computed by multiplying the standard hours per unit of output by the actual output of the period.

G. The last part of the chapter is concerned with fixed manufacturing overhead variances. Two variances are computed for fixed overhead—a budget variance and a volume variance.

1. The *fixed overhead budget variance,* or simply "budget variance," is the difference between actual fixed overhead costs and budgeted fixed overhead costs. The formula for the variance is:

$$\frac{\text{Budget}}{\text{variance}} = \frac{\text{Actual fixed}}{\text{overhead cost}} - \frac{\text{Budgeted fixed}}{\text{overhead cost}}$$

2. The formula for the *fixed overhead volume variance,* is:

$$\frac{\text{Volume}}{\text{variance}} = \frac{\text{Fixed}}{\text{overhead}} \times \left(\frac{\text{Denominator}}{\text{hours}} - \frac{\text{Standard}}{\text{hours}} \right)$$

The "fixed overhead rate" is the fixed portion of the predetermined overhead rate. The volume variance does not measure how well spending was controlled. It is completely determined by the relation between the denominator hours and the standard hours allowed for the actual output.

a. If the denominator activity is greater than the standard hours allowed for the output of the period, the volume variance is an unfavorable.

b. If the denominator activity is less than the standard hours allowed for the output of the period, the volume variance is favorable.

I. In a standard cost system, the amount of overhead applied to products is determined by the standard hours allowed for the actual output.

1. As in Chapter 2, if the actual overhead cost exceeds the amount of overhead cost applied to units of product, then the overhead is underapplied. If the actual overhead cost incurred is less than the amount of overhead cost applied to units, then the overhead is overapplied.

2. In a standard cost system, the sum of the overhead variances equals the amount of underapplied or overapplied overhead.

Overhead underapplied or overapplied =
   Variable overhead spending variance
 + Variable overhead efficiency variance
 + Fixed overhead budget variance
 + Fixed overhead volume variance

If the sum of the variances is unfavorable, the overhead is underapplied. If the sum of the variances is favorable, the overhead is overapplied.

REVIEW AND SELF-TEST
Questions and Exercises

True or False

Enter a T or an F in the blank to indicate whether the statement is true or false.

__T__ 1. A budget prepared for a single level of activity is called a static budget.

__F__ 2. Fixed costs are not controllable and therefore should be omitted from performance reports.

__F__ 3. A manger should be judged on the basis of how well he or she is able to keep costs to their originally budgeted levels.

__F__ 4. Direct labor cost would generally be a better base to use in preparing a flexible budget than direct labor-hours.

__T__ 5. A variable overhead spending variance is affected by waste and excessive usage as well as price differentials.

__T__ 6. The term "overhead efficiency variance" is really a misnomer since this variance has nothing to do with efficiency in the use of overhead.

__T__ 7. If overhead is applied to production on the basis of direct labor-hours, the labor efficiency variance and the overhead efficiency variance will always be favorable or unfavorable together.

__F__ 8. The fixed overhead volume variance measures how well fixed overhead spending was controlled.

__F__ 9. If the denominator activity level exceeds the standard hours allowed for the output, the volume variance will be favorable.

__T__ 10. In a standard cost system, if overhead is overapplied, then the sum of the four manufacturing overhead variances will be favorable.

Multiple Choice

Choose the best answer or response by placing the identifying letter in the space provided.

__B__ 1. In a standard cost system, overhead is applied to production on the basis of: a) the actual hours required to complete the output of the period; b) the standard hours allowed to complete the output of the period; c) the denominator hours chosen for the period; d) none of these.

__C__ 2. If the standard hours allowed for the output of a period exceed the denominator hours used in setting overhead rates, there will be: a) a favorable budget variance; b) an unfavorable budget variance; c) a favorable volume variance; d) an unfavorable volume variance.

____ 3. Baxter Company uses a standard cost system in which manufacturing overhead is applied to units of product on the basis of direct labor-hours. The variable portion of the company's predetermined overhead rate is $3 per direct labor-hour. The standards call for 2 direct labor-hours per unit of output. In March, the company produced 2,000 units using 4,100 direct labor-hours and the actual variable overhead cost incurred was $12,050. What was the variable overhead spending variance? a) $250 U; b) $250 F; c) $6,050 U; d) $6,050 F.

____ 4. Refer to the data in part (3) above concerning Baxter Company. What was the variable overhead efficiency variance for March? a) $6,300 F; b) $6,300 U; c) $300 F; d) $300 U.

____ 5. Baxter Company's flexible budget for manufacturing overhead indicates that the fixed overhead should be $30,000 at the denominator level of 3,000 standard direct labor-hours. In March, the actual fixed overhead cost incurred was $33,000. Recall from the above data concerning Baxter Company that the standards call for 2 direct labor-hours per unit of output and that in March, the company produced 2,000 units using 4,100 direct labor-hours (DLHs). What is the fixed portion of the predetermined overhead rate? a) $10 per DLH; b) $11 per DLH; c) $30 per DLH; d) $2 per DLH.

___ 6. Refer to the data in parts (3) and (5) above concerning Baxter Company. How much overhead (both variable and fixed) was applied to units of product during March? a) $12,000; b) $30,000; c) $52,000; d) $42,000.

___ 7. Refer to the data in part (5) above concerning Baxter Company. What was the fixed overhead budget variance for March? a) $10,000 F; b) $10,000 U; c) $3,000 U; d) $3,000 F.

___ 8. Refer to the data in part (5) above concerning Baxter Company. What was the fixed overhead volume variance for March? a) $10,000 F; b) $10,000 U; c) $3,000 U; d) $3,000 F.

Exercises

9-1. Herbold Corporation uses the following cost formulas in its flexible budget for manufacturing overhead:

Item	Cost Formula
Utilities	$6,000 per year, plus $0.30 per machine-hour (MH)
Supplies	$10,000 per year, plus $0.80 per machine-hour
Depreciation	$25,000 per year
Indirect labor	$21,000 per year, plus $0.40 per machine-hour

Using these cost formulas, complete the following flexible budget:

Overhead Costs	Cost Formula (per MH)	Machine-hours 8,000	10,000	12,000
Variable overhead costs:				
Utilities	0.30	2400	3000	3600
Supplies	0.80	6400	8000	9600
Indirect labor	0.40	3200	4000	4800
Total variable overhead costs	1.50	12000	15000	18000
Fixed overhead costs:				
Depreciation		25000	25000	25000
		6000	6000	6000
		10,000	10000	10000
		21000	21000	21000
Total fixed overhead costs		62000	62000	62000
Total overhead costs		74000	77000	98000

9-2.   Refer to the flexible budget data in Exercise 9-1. The standard time to complete one unit of product is 1.6 machine-hours. Last year the company budgeted to operate at the 10,000 machine-hour level of activity. During the year the following actual activity took place:

Number of units produced..............................	5,000 units
Actual machine-hours worked.......................	8,500 hours

Actual overhead costs:

	Variable	Fixed
Utilities...............................	$2,600	$5,900
Supplies...............................	$6,700	$10,300
Indirect labor.......................	$3,300	$21,700
Depreciation........................		$25,000

Prepare a performance report for the year using the format that appears below. Do not compute efficiency variances for variable overhead items.

Performance Report
Herbold Corporation

Budgeted machine-hours.............................	10,000
Actual machine-hours	8500
Standard machine-hours.............................	8000

	Cost Formula (per MH)	Actual Costs 8,500 MHs	Budget Based on 8500 MHs	Spending or Budget Variance
Variable overhead costs:				
Utilities	0.30	2600	2550	50 U
Supplies	0.80	6700	6800	100 F
I.L	0.40	3300	3400	100 F
Total variable overhead costs		12600	12750	150 F
Fixed overhead costs:				
		5900	6000	
		10300		
		21700		
		25000		
Total fixed overhead costs		62900	62000	62900 U
Total overhead costs				

9-3. The flexible budget for manufacturing overhead for Marina Company is given below:

Marina Company
Flexible Budget

Overhead Costs	*Cost Formula (per DLH)*	*Direct Labor-hours* 10,000	12,000	14,000
Variable overhead costs:				
Electricity	$0.15	$ 1,500	$ 1,800	$ 2,100
Indirect materials	0.50	5,000	6,000	7,000
Indirect labor	0.25	2,500	3,000	3,500
Total variable overhead costs	$0.90	9,000	10,800	12,600
Fixed overhead costs:				
Depreciation		11,500	11,500	11,500
Property taxes		8,500	8,500	8,500
Insurance		4,000	4,000	4,000
Total fixed overhead costs		24,000	24,000	24,000
Total overhead costs		$33,000	$34,800	$36,600

Marina Company uses a standard cost system in which manufacturing overhead is applied to units of product on the basis of direct labor-hours (DLHs). A denominator activity level of 12,000 direct labor-hours is used in setting predetermined overhead rates. The standard time to complete one unit of product is 1.5 direct labor-hours.

For the company's most recent year, the following actual operating data are available:

Units produced	9,000 units
Actual direct labor-hours worked	14,000 DLHs
Actual variable overhead cost	$12,880
Actual fixed overhead cost	$23,750

a. Compute the predetermined overhead rate that would be used by the company, and break it down into variable and fixed cost elements:

Predetermined overhead rate	2.90
Variable cost element	0.90
Fixed cost element	2

b. How much overhead would have been applied to work in process during the year? 39150

c. Complete the following variance analysis of variable overhead cost for the company's most recent year (see Chapter 8):

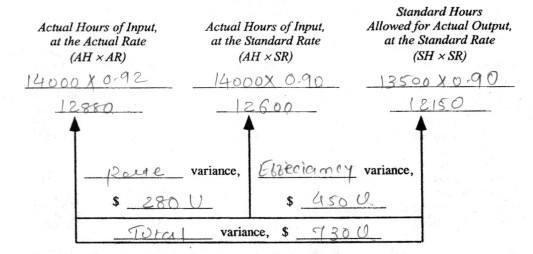

Actual Hours of Input, at the Actual Rate (AH × AR)	Actual Hours of Input, at the Standard Rate (AH × SR)	Standard Hours Allowed for Actual Output, at the Standard Rate (SH × SR)
14000 X 0·92	14000X 0.90	13500 X 0·90
12880	12600	12150

Rate variance, $ 280 U   Efficiency variance, $ 450 U

Total variance, $ 730 U

d. Complete the following variance analysis of fixed overhead cost for the company's most recent year:

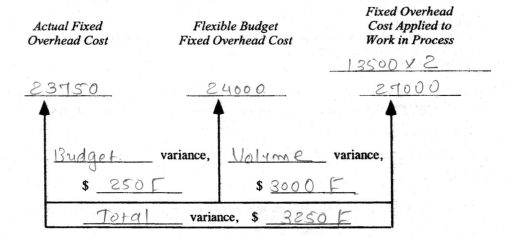

Actual Fixed Overhead Cost	Flexible Budget Fixed Overhead Cost	Fixed Overhead Cost Applied to Work in Process
		13500 X 2
23750	24000	27000

Budget variance, $ 250 F   Volume variance, $ 3000 F

Total variance, $ 3250 F

Answers to Questions and Exercises

True or False

1. T A static budget is prepared for only one level of activity.

2. F Many fixed costs are controllable and must be on someone's performance report or no one will attempt to control them.

3. F This may be true in government, but is not true in commercial enterprises. Costs will be higher or lower than budgeted simply due to changes in activity. It is unreasonable to expect, for example, that a production manager will be able to make 10% more units than budgeted (if requested by marketing) without spending more than was originally budgeted.

4. F It is generally best to avoid using dollars in the activity base.

5. T The overhead spending variance contains elements of both price and quantity variances.

6. T The overhead efficiency variance really reflects efficiency in the base underlying the application of overhead.

7. T The reason for the close relationship is that both variances are based on the difference between the actual direct labor-hours and the standard direct labor-hours allowed for the actual output.

8. F The fixed overhead volume variance results from a difference between the denominator level of activity and the standard hours allowed for the actual output of the period. It has nothing to do with spending.

9. F The reverse is true—the volume variance would be unfavorable.

10. T Overapplied overhead is equivalent to favorable variances and underapplied overhead is equivalent to unfavorable variances.

Multiple Choice

1. b This point is illustrated in Exhibit 9-9.

2. c The volume variance is favorable any time the standard hours allowed for the actual output of the period exceeds the denominator level of activity.

3. b
Spending var. $= (AH \times AR) - (AH \times SR)$
$= (\$12,050) - (4,100 \times \$3)$
$= \$250$ F

4. d
Efficiency var. $= (AH \times SR) - (SH \times SR)$
$= (4,100 \times \$3) - (4,000^* \times \$3)$
$= \$300$ U
* 2,000 units $\times$ 2 DLHs per unit = 4,000 DLHs

5. a
$$\text{Fixed portion of the predetermined overhead rate} = \frac{\$30,000}{3,000 \text{ DLHs}}$$
$$= \$10 \text{ per DLH}$$

6. c
$$\text{Prdetermined overhead rate} = \$3 + \$10$$
$$= \$13 \text{ per DLH}$$
$$\text{Standard hours allowed for the output} = \frac{2,000}{\text{units}} \times \frac{2 \text{ DLHs}}{\text{per unit}}$$
$$= 4,000 \text{ DLHs}$$
Overhead applied $= \$13 \times 4,000$
$= \$52,000$

7. c
$$\text{Budget variance} = \text{Actual fixed overhead cost} - \text{Budgeted fixed overhead cost}$$
$$= \$33,000 - \$30,000$$
$$= \$3,000 \text{ U}$$

8. a
$$\text{Volume variance} = \text{Fixed overhead rate} \times \left(\text{Denominator hours} - \text{Standard hours allowed} \right)$$
$$= \$10 \times (3,000 - 4,000) = \$10,000 \text{ F}$$

Exercises

9-1.

Overhead Costs	Cost Formula (per MH)	Machine-hours		
		8,000	10,000	12,000
Variable overhead costs:				
Utilities	$0.30	$ 2,400	$ 3,000	$ 3,600
Supplies	0.80	6,400	8,000	9,600
Indirect labor	0.40	3,200	4,000	4,800
Total variable overhead costs	$1.50	12,000	15,000	18,000
Fixed overhead costs:				
Utilities		6,000	6,000	6,000
Supplies		10,000	10,000	10,000
Depreciation		25,000	25,000	25,000
Indirect labor		21,000	21,000	21,000
Total fixed overhead costs		62,000	62,000	62,000
Total overhead costs		$74,000	$77,000	$80,000

9-2.

Performance Report
Herbold Corporation

Budgeted machine-hours	10,000
Actual machine-hours	8,500
Standard machine-hours	8,000

	Cost Formula (per MH)	Actual Costs 8,500 MHs	Budget Based on 8,500 MHs	Spending or Budget Variance
Variable overhead costs:				
Utilities	$0.30	$ 2,600	$ 2,550	$ 50 U
Supplies	0.80	6,700	6,800	100 F
Indirect labor	0.40	3,300	3,400	100 F
Total variable overhead costs	$1.50	12,600	12,750	150 F
Fixed overhead costs:				
Utilities		5,900	6,000	100 F
Supplies		10,300	10,000	300 U
Depreciation		25,000	25,000	--
Indirect labor		21,700	21,000	700 U
Total fixed overhead costs		62,900	62,000	900 U
Total overhead costs		$75,500	$74,750	$750 U

9-3.   a.   Predetermined overhead rate ($34,800 ÷ 12,000 DLHs) $2.90 per DLH
Variable element ($10,800 ÷ 12,000 DLHs) $0.90 per DLH
Fixed element ($24,000 ÷ 12,000 DLHs) $2.00 per DLH

b.   Overhead applied:
9,000 units × 1.5 DLHs per unit = 13,500 DLHs allowed
13,500 DLHs × $2.90 per DLH = $39,150 overhead applied

c.   Variable overhead variance analysis:

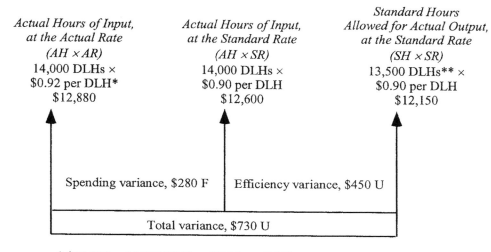

Actual Hours of Input, at the Actual Rate *(AH × AR)*	Actual Hours of Input, at the Standard Rate *(AH × SR)*	*Standard Hours Allowed for Actual Output,* at the Standard Rate *(SH × SR)*
14,000 DLHs × $0.92 per DLH*	14,000 DLHs × $0.90 per DLH	13,500 DLHs** × $0.90 per DLH
$12,880	$12,600	$12,150

Spending variance, $280 F   Efficiency variance, $450 U

Total variance, $730 U

* $12,880 ÷ 14,000 DLHs = $0.92 per DLH
** 9,000 units × 1.5 DLHs per unit = 13,500 DLHs

d.   Fixed overhead variance analysis:

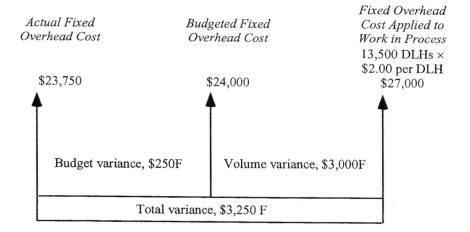

Actual Fixed Overhead Cost	*Budgeted Fixed Overhead Cost*	*Fixed Overhead Cost Applied to Work in Process*
		13,500 DLHs × $2.00 per DLH
$23,750	$24,000	$27,000

Budget variance, $250F   Volume variance, $3,000F

Total variance, $3,250 F

Chapter 10

Decentralization

Chapter Study Suggestions

This relatively brief chapter covers general concepts of decentralization and two measures of performance that are commonly used in investment centers—return on investment (ROI) and residual income. Memorize the formulas for ROI and residual income since they are used extensively in homework.

CHAPTER HIGHLIGHTS

A. A *responsibility accounting* system functions best in a decentralized organization. A *decentralized organization* is one in which decision-making is spread throughout the organization, with managers at all levels making decisions. In a decentralized organization the responsibility accounting system is structured around cost centers, profit centers, and investment centers.

　1. A *cost center* is a responsibility center where a manager has control over cost but not over revenues or investments. A cost center manager is usually held responsible for minimizing cost while providing quality goods and services as requested.

　2. The manager of a *profit center* has control over both cost and revenue. A profit center manager is usually held responsible for maximizing profit.

　3. The manager of an *investment center* has control over cost, revenue, and investments in operating assets. An investment center manager is ordinarily evaluated on the basis of return on investment or residual income, as explained later.

B. Investment center performance is often measured by *return on investment (ROI),* which is defined as:

$$ROI = \frac{\text{Net operating income}}{\text{Average operating assets}}$$

The ROI can also be expressed in terms of margin and turnover:

$$ROI = Margin \times Turnover$$

where:

$$Margin = \frac{\text{Net operating income}}{\text{Sales}}$$

$$Turnover = \frac{\text{Sales}}{\text{Average operating assets}} .$$

　1. *Net operating income* is income before interest and taxes.

　2. *Operating assets* include cash, accounts receivable, inventory, and all other assets held for productive use within the organization. Operating assets do *not* include, for example, investments in other companies and investments in undeveloped land. Assets that are common to all divisions (such as assets associated with corporate headquarters) should not be allocated to the divisions when making ROI computations.

　3. Holding all other things constant, a company's return on investment can be improved by increasing sales, reducing expenses, or reducing assets.

　4. ROI is criticized for several reasons. One of the most important criticisms is that a division manager who is evaluated based on ROI will tend to reject projects whose ROIs are less than the division's current ROI but greater than the company's minimum rate of return. Rejecting such a project would not be in the best interests of the company since a project whose rate of return exceeds the minimum rate of return should ordinarily be accepted.

C. Residual income is another approach to measuring performance in an investment center.

　1. *Residual income* is the net operating income that an investment center earns above the minimum required rate of return on operating assets.

$$\begin{matrix} \text{Residual} \\ \text{income} \end{matrix} = \begin{matrix} \text{Net} \\ \text{operating} - \\ \text{income} \end{matrix} \left(\begin{matrix} \text{Required} & \text{Average} \\ \text{rate of} & \times \text{operating} \\ \text{return} & \text{assets} \end{matrix} \right)$$

　2. The residual income approach to performance evaluation encourages investment in worthwhile projects that would be rejected under ROI.

　3. Unfortunately, the residual income approach can't be easily used to compare divisions of different sizes. Larger divisions naturally tend to have larger residual incomes than smaller divisions.

D. It is fairly common for one part of a company to provide goods or services to another part of the company. For example, the General Motors truck division sells delivery trucks to the Chevrolet Division. The price charged for such a sale inside a company is called a *transfer price.*

　1. If the divisions are profit or investment centers, then the selling division would like the transfer price to be high and the purchasing division would like the price to be low.

　2. The objective in setting transfer prices should be to encourage the managers to make decisions that are in the best interests of the overall organization.

REVIEW AND SELF-TEST
Questions and Exercises

True or False

Enter a T or an F in the blank to indicate whether the statement is true or false.

____ 1. A decentralized organization is one in which decision-making is confined to top management.

____ 2. Residual income is equal to the difference between total revenues and operating expenses.

____ 3. Using ROI to evaluate managers may lead managers to reject investment opportunities that would be beneficial to the company as a whole.

____ 4. A profit center manager is responsible for generating revenue, but is not responsible for controlling costs.

____ 5. A reduction in operating assets will increase a division's ROI if sales and expenses remain unchanged.

____ 6. In computing residual income, expenses incurred in operating corporate headquarters should be allocated to the separate divisions on the basis of the contribution margins of the divisions.

____ 7. Under the residual income approach, the manager should seek to maximize the rate of return on operating assets.

____ 8. An increase in total sales would typically increase turnover but would have no effect on margin.

Multiple Choice

Choose the best answer or response by placing the identifying letter in the space provided.

____ 1. If the level of inventory in a company is reduced, and if sales and expenses remain unchanged, one would expect the company's ROI to: a) increase; b) decrease; c) remain unchanged; d) it is impossible to tell what would happen to ROI.

____ 2. A company reported the following results:

Average operating assets	$45,000
Sales	$180,000
Contribution margin	$21,600
Net operating income	$9,000

The company's ROI would be: a) 48%; b) 12%; c) 20%; d) 30%.

____ 3. The objective of the residual income approach is to: a) maximize a segment's overall rate of return; b) maximize the ROI that a segment is able to get on its operating assets; c) maximize the total amount of the residual income; d) none of these.

____ 4. A company reported the following results:

Average operating assets	$300,000
Stockholders' equity	$50,000
Sales	$900,000
Net operating income	$75,000
Minimum required rate of return	18%

The company's residual income would be: a) $25,000; b) $15,000; c) $21,000; d) 475,000.

Chapter 10

Exercises

10-1. Frankel Company has the following data for its Connectors Division for last year:

Sales..	$2,000,000
Net operating income..................	$160,000
Average operating assets.............	$800,000
Minimum rate of return..............	16%

a. Compute the return on investment (ROI) for the Connectors Division, using margin and turnover.

$$ROI = \frac{160000}{800000}$$

$$= 20\%$$

b. Compute the residual income for the Connectors Division.

$$NOI - \left(\begin{array}{c} Required \\ Rate\ of\ Return \end{array} \times \begin{array}{c} Avg.\ operating \\ Assets \end{array} \right)$$

$$160000 - (16\% \times 800000)$$

$$= 160000 - 128000$$

$$= 32,000.$$

10-2. Fill in the missing information for the three different companies below:

	Company 1	Company 2	Company 3
Sales	$600,000	$600,000	$ 180000
Net operating income	$60,000	$45000	$27,000
Average operating assets	$300,000	$200,000	$100000
Margin...	10%	7.5%	15
Turnover	2	3	1.8
Return on investment (ROI)	20%	22.5	27%

ROI= Margin × T.O

$20\% = X \times 2$

$X =$

$Turnover = \frac{Sales}{A.O.A}$

$1.8 = \frac{Sales}{100000}$

$Sales?$

Margin: $\frac{NOI}{Sales}$

$7.5\% = \frac{NOI}{600000}$

$NOI = 600000 \times 7.5\%$

$Turnover = \frac{Sales}{A.O.A}$

$1.8 = \frac{Sales}{A.O.A}$

$ROI = \frac{NOI}{A.O.A}$

$27\% = \frac{27000}{A.O.A}$

$A.O.A = \frac{27000}{27\%}$

108

Answers to Questions and Exercises

True or False

1. F   In a decentralized organization, decision-making is spread through all levels of management.

2. F   Residual income is the difference between net operating income and the minimum return that should be earned on operating assets.

3. T   This is a major criticism of the ROI method.

4. F   A profit center is responsible for controlling costs as well as generating revenues.

5. T   A reduction in assets will result in an increase in turnover and an increase in ROI.

6. F   Common expenses, such as those associated with operating corporate headquarters, should not be allocated to segments when evaluating the performance of the segment managers.

7. F   Under the residual income approach, the manager should try to maximize residual income.

8. F   The margin would also typically increase, since the net operating income would generally increase more rapidly than sales due to the effects of operating leverage discussed in an earlier chapter.

Multiple Choice

1. a   If the level of inventory is reduced, then operating assets are reduced. The result will be higher turnover and an increase in the ROI.

2. c   The computations are:

$$\text{ROI} = \frac{\$9,000}{\$180,000} \times \frac{\$180,000}{\$45,000} = 5\% \times 4 = 20\%$$

3. c   Residual income has nothing to do with ROI; moreover, as residual income increases, ROI frequently decreases (as shown in examples in the chapter).

4. c   The computations are:

Average operating assets	$300,000
Net operating income	$ 75,000
Minimum required return (18% × $300,000)	54,000
Residual income	$ 21,000

Exercises

10-1. a. $\text{Margin} = \dfrac{\text{Net operating income}}{\text{Sales}} = \dfrac{\$160,000}{\$2,000,000} = 8\%$

$\text{Turnover} = \dfrac{\text{Sales}}{\text{Average operating assets}} = \dfrac{\$2,000,000}{\$800,000} = 2.5$

$\text{ROI} = \text{Margin} \times \text{Turnover}$
$\phantom{\text{ROI}} = 8\% \times 2.5 = 20\%$

b.
Average operating assets	$800,000
Net operating income............................	$160,000
Minimum required return	
(16% × $800,000)	128,000
Residual income..................................	$ 32,000

10-2.

	Company 1	Company 2	Company 3
Sales	$600,000*	$600,000*	$180,000
Net operating income	$60,000*	$45,000	$27,000*
Average operating assets	$300,000*	$200,000*	$100,000
Margin	10%	7.5%*	15%
Turnover	2	3.0	1.8*
Return on investment (ROI)	20%	22.5%	27%*

*Given

Chapter 11

Relevant Costs for Decision Making

Chapter Study Suggestions

The concept of relevant costs is covered in the first few pages of the chapter. Study these pages carefully, since this basic idea is used throughout the chapter.

A number of specific decision-making situations are covered in the chapter. The same principles are used in each situation to identify the relevant costs.

CHAPTER HIGHLIGHTS

A. Every decision involves a choice from among at least two alternatives. A *relevant cost* or benefit is a cost or benefit that differs between alternatives. If a cost or benefit does not differ between alternatives, it is not relevant in the decision and can be ignored. *Avoidable cost, differential cost,* and *incremental cost* are synonyms for relevant cost.

    1. Two broad classifications of costs are irrelevant in decisions: (a) sunk costs; and (b) future costs that do not differ between alternatives. *Sunk costs* are costs that have already been incurred and are irrevocable. Thus, they cannot differ between alternatives and are always irrelevant.

    2. To make a decision, you should:

        a. Eliminate the costs and benefits that do not differ between alternatives. These irrelevant costs consist of sunk costs and future costs that do not differ between alternatives.

        b. Make a decision based on the remaining cost and benefit data. These data consist of the costs and benefits that differ between alternatives.

    3. Costs that are relevant in one situation may not be relevant in another situation. There are no rules for identifying what costs are relevant and what costs are irrelevant except that costs that do not differ between alternatives are irrelevant.

B. You should disregard irrelevant costs and benefits in decisions for three reasons:

        a. In any given situation, the irrelevant costs greatly outnumber the relevant costs. Focusing just on the relevant costs simply takes less time and effort.

        b. The use of irrelevant costs intermingled with relevant costs may draw attention away from the really critical data.

        c. People often make mistakes when they include irrelevant costs in an analysis. For example, when dealing with fixed costs that are stated on a per unit basis, people often make the mistake of treating them as if they are variable costs that change with the number of units produced and sold changes.

C. *Adding or dropping a segment* such as a product line is one of the decision-making situations covered in the chapter. In making this decision, compare the contribution margin of the segment to the fixed costs that could be avoided by dropping the segment.

    1. If the contribution margin lost by dropping a segment is greater than the fixed costs that can be avoided, then the segment should be retained.

    2. If the contribution margin lost by dropping a segment is less than the fixed costs that can be avoided, then the segment should be dropped.

    3. Exhibit 11-3 illustrates an alternative approach to deciding whether to retain or drop a product line or other segment of a company. In this approach two income statements are prepared—one for each alternative.

    4. The decision to keep or drop a product line or other segment of a company is often clouded by the allocation of common fixed costs.

        a. Allocations of common costs can make a product line or other segment *appear* to be unprofitable, when in fact the segment may be contributing substantially to the overall profits of the company.

        b. Common fixed costs should never be allocated to segments of a company; segments should be charged only with those costs that are directly traceable to them, as shown in Exhibit 11-4.

D. A decision to produce a part internally rather than to buy it from a supplier is called a *make or buy decision*. The relevant costs in such a decision, as always, are the costs that differ between the alternatives.

    1. Exhibit 11-5 contains an example of a make or buy decision. Notice from the exhibit that the costs that are relevant in a make or buy decision are the costs that *differ* between the make or buy alternatives.

    2. Opportunity cost may be a key factor in a make or buy decision as well as in other decisions.

        a. If the resources that are currently being used to make a part or a product all have excess capacity, then the opportunity cost is zero.

        b. On the other hand, if buying from outside the company would release capacity that could be used to produce something else that customers will pay for, then there is an opportunity cost. This opportunity cost is the segment margin that could be obtained from the alternative use of the capacity. The opportunity cost should be included in the analysis.

E. Another decision concerns *special orders*—one-time orders that don't affect regular sales. For example, a company may receive an order on a one-time basis from an overseas customer in a market the company does not ordinarily sell in. Such a special order should be accepted if the incremental revenue from the special order exceeds the incremental (i.e., avoidable) costs of the order. Any opportunity costs should be taken into account.

F. A *constraint* is anything that limits the organization's ability to further its goals. When demand exceeds capacity and the constraint is a machine or a workstation, it is called a *bottleneck*. For example, a company may be able to sell 1,000 units of a product per week, but the product may require a machine that is capable of only producing 800 units a week. The machine would be a bottleneck.

1. When demand exceeds capacity, a production constraint of some sort exists. In that case, managers must decide what the company will *not* do since it cannot do everything.

2. The problem is how to best utilize a constrained resource. The company cannot do everything—it must decide what it will and will not do. Fixed costs are likely to be unaffected by this decision and therefore are irrelevant. If the fixed costs are constant and irrelevant, maximizing the company's total contribution margin is equivalent to maximizing the company's profit. Given capacity and the company's fixed costs, the problem is how to best use that capacity to maximize total contribution margin and profit.

3. The key to the efficient utilization of a scarce resource is *the contribution margin per unit of the constrained resource*. The products with the greatest contribution margin per unit of the constrained resource are the most profitable; they generate the greatest profit from a given amount of the constrained resource. These products should be emphasized over products with a lower contribution margin per unit of the constrained resource.

4. Since the constraint limits the output of the entire organization, increasing the amount of the constrained resource can yield a huge payoff. This is called "elevating the constraint" and can be accomplished in a variety of ways including working overtime on the bottleneck, buying another machine, subcontracting work, and so on.

5. The contribution margin per unit of the constrained resource is also a measure of opportunity cost. For example, when considering whether to accept an order for a product that uses the constrained resource, the opportunity cost of using the constrained resource should be considered. That opportunity cost is the lost contribution margin for the job that would be displaced if the order were accepted.

REVIEW AND SELF-TEST
Questions and Exercises

True or False

Enter a T or an F in the blank to indicate whether the statement is true or false.

____ 1. All costs are relevant in a decision except costs that do not differ between alternatives.

____ 2. In a decision, variable costs are relevant costs and fixed costs are irrelevant.

____ 3. Sunk costs may be relevant in a decision.

____ 4. Future costs are always relevant in decision-making.

____ 5. Costs that are relevant in one decision are not necessarily relevant in another decision.

____ 6. If a company is able to avoid more in fixed costs than it loses in contribution margin by dropping a product, then it will be better off financially if the product is eliminated.

____ 7. Allocation of common fixed costs to product lines and to other segments of a company helps the manager to see if the product line or segment is profitable.

____ 8. If a product has a negative segment margin, the product should be discontinued.

____ 9. Opportunity cost may be a key factor in a make or buy decision.

____ 10. If there is a constrained resource, a company should emphasize the product that has the highest contribution margin per unit.

Multiple Choice

Choose the best answer or response by placing the identifying letter in the space provided.

____ 1. All of the following costs are relevant in a make or buy decision except: a) the opportunity cost of space; b) costs that are avoidable by buying rather than making; c) variable costs of producing the item; d) costs that are differential between the make and buy alternatives; e) all of the above costs are relevant.

____ 2. One of Simplex Company's products has a contribution margin of $50,000 and fixed costs totaling $60,000. If the product is dropped, $40,000 of the fixed costs will continue unchanged. As a result of dropping the product, the company's net operating income should: a) decrease by $50,000; b) increase by $30,000; c) decrease by $30,000; d) increase by $10,000.

____ 3. Halley Company produces 2,000 parts each year that are used in one of its products. The unit product cost of this part is:

Variable manufacturing cost	$ 7.50
Fixed manufacturing cost	6.00
Unit product cost	$13.50

The part can be purchased from an outside supplier for $10 per unit. If the part is purchased from the outside supplier, two-thirds of the fixed manufacturing costs can be eliminated. The effect on net operating income from purchasing the part would be a: a) $3,000 increase; b) $1,000 decrease; c) $7,000 increase; d) $5,000 decrease.

____ 4. Product A has a contribution margin of $8 per unit, a contribution margin ratio of 50%, and requires 4 machine-hours to produce. Product B has a contribution margin of $12 per unit, a contribution margin ratio of 40%, and requires 5 machine-hours to produce. If the constraint is machine-hours, then the company should emphasize: a) Product A; b) Product B.

____ 5. Sunderson Products, Inc. has received a special order for 1,000 units of a sport-fighting kite. The customer has offered a price of $9.95 for each kite. The unit costs of the kite, at its normal sales level of 30,000 units per year, are detailed below:

Variable production costs	$5.25
Fixed production costs	2.35
Variable selling costs	0.75
Fixed selling and admin. costs	3.45

There is ample idle capacity to produce the special order without any increase in total fixed costs. The variable selling costs on the special order would be $0.15 per unit instead of $0.75 per unit. The special order would have no impact on the company's other sales. What effect would accepting this special order have on the company's net operating income? a) $1,850 increase; b) $1,850 decrease; c) $4,550 increase; d) $4,550 decrease.

Exercises

11-1.   The most recent income statement for the men's formal wear department of Merrill's Department Store is given below:

Sales		$500,000
Less variable expenses		200,000
Contribution margin		300,000
Less fixed expenses:		
Salaries and wages	$150,000	
Insurance on inventories	10,000	
Depreciation of fixtures	65,000*	
Advertising	100,000	325,000
Net operating income (loss)		$ (25,000)

*Six year remaining useful life, with little or no current resale value.

Due to its poor showing, management is thinking about dropping the men's formal wear department. If the department is dropped, a make-work position will be found for one long-time employee who is due to retire in several years. That employee's salary is $30,000. The fixtures in the department would have no resale value and would be hauled to the county dump.
    Prepare an analysis, using the following form, to determine whether the department should be dropped.

Contribution margin lost if the department is dropped .... $ _____

Less avoidable fixed costs:

_____ .... $ _____

_____ ....   _____

_____ ....   _____   _____

Increase (decrease) in operating income .... $_____

Based on this analysis, should the men's formal wear department be dropped?

Redo the analysis, using the alternate format shown below:

	Keep Department	Drop Department	Difference: Income Increase (Decrease)
Sales	$500,000	$_____	$_____
Less variable expenses	200,000	_____	_____
Contribution margin	300,000	_____	_____
Less fixed expenses:			
Salaries and wages	150,000	_____	_____
Insurance on inventories	10,000	_____	_____
Depreciation of equipment	65,000	_____	_____
Advertising	100,000	_____	_____
Total fixed expenses	325,000	_____	_____
Net operating income (loss)	$ (25,000)	$_____	$_____

11-2.   Petre Company is now making a small part that is used in one of its products. The company's accounting department reports the following costs of producing the part internally:

	Per Part
Direct materials	$15
Direct labor	10
Variable manufacturing overhead	2
Fixed manufacturing overhead, traceable	4
Fixed manufacturing overhead, allocated common	5
Unit product cost	$36

A total of 75% of the traceable fixed manufacturing overhead cost consists of depreciation of special equipment, and 25% consists of supervisory salaries. The special equipment has no resale value. The supervisory salaries could be avoided if production of the part were discontinued.

   An outside supplier has offered to sell the parts to Petre Company for $30 each, based on an order of 5,000 parts per year. Should Petre Company accept this offer, or continue to make the parts internally? Assume that direct labor is a variable cost. Use the following form in your answer:

	Relevant Costs for 5,000 Parts	
	Make	Buy
Outside purchase price		$_____
Cost of making internally:		
_____	$_____	
_____	_____	
_____	_____	
_____	_____	
_____	_____	
Total cost	$_____	$_____

11-3. Kuski Corporation makes two models of its hair dryer at a facility in Lexington. The copper-winding machine has been the constraint in the factory in the past. The capacity of this machine is 9,600 minutes per month. Data concerning these two products appear below:

	Standard	Premium
Unit selling price	$14.00	$20.00
Variable cost per unit	5.00	8.00
Copper-winding machine time per unit	0.5 minute	0.6 minute
Monthly demand	12,000 units	8,000 units

a. Determine if the copper-winding machine is currently a constraint. In other words, does demand exceed capacity? Use the form below to answer this question

	Standard	Premium	Total
....			
....			
Copper-winding time required to satisfy demand			

b. Compute the contribution margin per copper-winding minute for the two products using the following form:

	Standard	Premium
Unit selling price		
Variable cost per unit		
Contribution margin per unit		
Copper-winding machine time per unit		
Contribution margin per minute		

c. Assuming that the copper-winding machine is the company's constraint, how many units of each product should be made in order to maximize net operating income?

Answers to Questions and Exercises

True or False

1. T Costs that differ between alternatives are relevant. Costs that do not differ between alternatives are not relevant.

2. F Fixed costs can be relevant and variable costs can be irrelevant. What is relevant and what is irrelevant depends on the situation.

3. F Sunk costs are never relevant since they have already been incurred and thus can't be avoided by choosing one alternative over another.

4. F Future costs are relevant only if they differ between alternatives; future costs that do not differ between alternatives are irrelevant.

5. T For example, a product line manager's salary would be relevant in a decision to drop the product line, but would not be relevant in a decision about how much to spend on advertising.

6. T If the avoidable fixed costs exceed the lost contribution margin, profits would increase if the product line were dropped.

7. F Allocation of common fixed costs to product lines and to other segments of a company can easily result in misleading data and can make a product line appear to be unprofitable when in fact it may be one of a company's best products.

8. F Even if a product line has a negative segment margin, the product's costs must still be analyzed to determine if the product should be dropped. For example, depreciation on special equipment with no resale value would be traceable to the product line, but would not be relevant in a decision to drop the product line.

9. T Opportunity cost can be a key factor in *any* decision involving a constrained resource.

10. F The product with the highest contribution margin per unit of the constrained resource should be emphasized. A product might have a high contribution margin per unit but require a disproportionately large amount of the constrained resource.

Multiple Choice

1. e These costs are all relevant because they all differ between the alternatives.

2. c The computations are:

Contribution margin lost.................. $(50,000)
Less avoidable fixed costs 20,000*
Decrease in operating income.......... $(30,000)
*$60,000 – $40,000 = $20,000

3. a The computations are:

	Differential Cost	
	Make	Buy
Variable manuf. costs	$ 7.50	—
Avoidable fixed manufacturing cost.........	4.00	—
Outside purchase price........	—	$10.00
Total relevant cost..............	$11.50	$10.00

2,000 units × $1.50 = $3,000

4. b The computations are:

	A	B
Contribution margin per unit (a)..................	$8.00	$12.00
Machine-hours to produce (b).................	4.00	5.00
CM per machine-hour (a) ÷ (b)	$2.00	$ 2.40

5. c The computations are:

Incremental revenue
        ($9.95 × 1,000) $9,950
Incremental costs:
        Variable production
        ($5.25 × 1,000) 5,250
        Variable selling
        ($0.15 × 1,000) 150
Increase in operating income $4,550

Exercises

11-1.

Contribution margin lost if the department is dropped		$(300,000)
Less avoidable fixed costs:		
Salaries and wages ($150,000 - $30,000)	$120,000	
Insurance on inventories	10,000	
Advertising	100,000	230,000
Decrease in overall company net operating income.....................		$ (70,000)

Based on the analysis above, the department should not be dropped. The solution using the alternate format appears below:

	Keep Department	Drop Department	Difference: Income Increase or (Decrease)
Sales	$500,000	$ 0	$(500,000)
Less variable expenses	200,000	0	200,000
Contribution margin	300,000	0	$(300,000)
Less fixed expenses:			
Salaries and wages	150,000	30,000	120,000
Insurance on inventories...............................	10,000	0	10,000
Depreciation of fixtures...............................	65,000	65,000*	0
Advertising...	100,000	0	100,000
Total fixed expenses..	325,000	95,000	230,000
Net operating income (loss).............................	$(25,000)	$(95,000)	$ (70,000)

* If the department were dropped, the remaining book value of the fixtures would be written off immediately. If the department were not dropped, the remaining book value would be written off over a number of years in the form of depreciation charges. In either case, the entire remaining book value will eventually flow through the income statement as charges in one form or another.

11-2.

	Relevant Costs for 5,000 Parts	
	Make	Buy
Outside purchase price..		$150,000
Cost of making internally:		
Direct materials	$ 75,000	
Direct labor..	50,000	
Variable manufacturing overhead	10,000	
Fixed manufacturing overhead, traceable........................	5,000	
Fixed manufacturing overhead, allocated common.........		
Total..	$140,000	$150,000
Difference in favor of making...	$10,000	

The depreciation on the equipment and the common fixed overhead would not be avoidable costs.

11-3.

a. Demand exceeds capacity for the copper-winding machine, as shown below:

	Standard	*Premium*	*Total*
Monthly demand (a)	12,000 units	8,000 units	
Copper-winding machine time per unit (b)............	0.5 min./unit	0.6 min./unit	
Copper-winding time required			
to satisfy demand (a) × (b).................................	6,000 min.	4,800 min.	10,800 min.

b.

	Standard	*Premium*
Unit selling price	$14.00	$20.00
Variable cost per unit...	5.00	8.00
Contribution margin per unit (a).............................	$ 9.00	$12.00
Copper-winding machine time per unit (b)............	0.5 min.	0.6 min.
Contribution margin per minute (a) ÷ (b)	$ 18/min.	$ 20/min.

c. Since the contribution margin per copper-winding minute is higher for the premium model than for the standard model, the premium model should be emphasized. The optimal plan is to produce all 8,000 units of the premium model and use the remaining capacity to make 9,600 units of the standard model.

Total copper-winding time available..	9,600 minutes
Time required to produce 8,000 units of the premium model	4,800 minutes
Time remaining with which to make the standard model (a)	4,800 minutes
Time required to make one unit of the standard model (b)	0.5 minute/unit
Number of units of the standard model produced (a) ÷ (b)	9,600 units

Chapter 12

Capital Budgeting Decisions

Chapter Study Suggestions

You must have a solid understanding of the concept of present value before beginning this chapter. If you have not worked with present value before, carefully study Appendix 12A, "The Concept of Present Value," before starting on the chapter itself.

Once you understand present value, you will be ready to tackle the capital budgeting methods in the chapter. The first of these methods is called the net present value method. Follow through each number in Exhibits 12-1 and 12-2 and trace the factors back to the tables given at the end of the chapter.

Two other methods of making capital budgeting decisions are presented in detail in the chapter. These are the payback method and the simple rate of return method. Formulas are provided for both methods. Pay particular attention to the formula for the simple rate of return—it can be tricky to apply.

CHAPTER HIGHLIGHTS

A. The term *capital budgeting* is used to describe planning major outlays on projects that commit the company for some time into the future such as purchasing new equipment, building a new facility, or introducing a new product.

    1. Capital budgeting usually involves investment; i.e., committing funds now so as to obtain cash inflows in the future.

    2. Capital budgeting decisions fall into two broad categories:

        a. *Screening decisions:* Potential projects are categorized as acceptable or unacceptable.

        b. *Preference decisions*: Projects must be ranked because funds are insufficient to support all of the acceptable projects.

    3. The time value of money should be considered. A dollar in the future is worth less than a dollar today for the simple reason that a dollar today can be invested to yield more than a dollar in the future.

        a. *Discounted cash flow methods* give full recognition to the time value of money.

        b. Two methods involve discounting cash flows—the *net present value method* and the *internal rate of return method*.

B. The net present value method is illustrated in Example A (Exhibit 12-1) and in Example B (Exhibit 12-2). The basic steps in this method are:

    1. Determine the required investment.

    2. Determine the future cash inflows and outflows that result from the investment.

    3. Use the *present value tables* to find the appropriate *present value factors*.

        a. The values (or factors) in the present value tables depend on the discount rate and the number of periods (usually years).

        b. The *discount rate* in present value analysis is the company's required rate of return, which is often the company's cost of capital. The *cost of capital* is the average rate of return the company must pay its long-term creditors and shareholders for the use of their funds. The details of the cost of capital are covered in finance courses.

    4. Multiply each cash flow by the appropriate present value factor and then sum the results. The end result (which is net of the initial investment) is called the *net present value* of the project.

    5. In a screening decision, if the net present value is positive, the investment is acceptable. If the net present value is negative, the investment should be rejected.

C. Discounted cash flow analysis is based entirely on *cash flows*—not on accounting net income. Accounting net income is ignored in cash flow analysis.

    1. Typical cash flows associated with an investment are:

        a. Outflows: initial investment (including installation costs); increased working capital needs; repairs and maintenance; and incremental operating costs.

        b. Inflows: incremental revenues; reductions in costs; salvage value; and release of working capital at the end of the project.

    2. Depreciation is not a cash flow and therefore is not part of the analysis. (However, depreciation can affect taxes, which is a cash flow. This aspect of depreciation is covered in more advanced texts.)

    3. Quite often, a project requires an infusion of cash (i.e., working capital) to finance inventories, receivables, and other working capital items. Typically, at the end of the project these working capital items can be liquidated (i.e., the inventory can be sold) and the cash that had been invested in these items can be recovered. Thus, working capital is counted as a cash outflow at the beginning of a project and as a cash inflow at the end of the project.

    4. We usually assume that all cash flows, other than the initial investment, occur at the *end* of a period.

D. The internal rate of return method is another discounted cash flow method used in capital budgeting decisions. The *internal rate of return* is the rate of return promised by an investment project over its useful life; it is the discount rate for which the net present value of a project is zero. The details of the internal rate of return method are covered in more advanced texts.

E. The *total-cost* approach or the *incremental-cost* approach can be used to compare projects.

    1. The total-cost approach is the most flexible method. Exhibit 12-3 shows this approach. Note in Exhibit 12-3 that *all* cash inflows and *all* cash outflows are included in the solution under each alternative.

2. The incremental-cost approach is a simpler and more direct route to a decision since it ignores all cash flows that are the same under both alternatives. Exhibit 12-4 shows this approach.

3. The total-cost and incremental-cost approaches lead to the same decision.

F. Sometimes no revenue or cash inflow is directly involved in a decision. In this situation, the alternative with the *least cost* should be selected. The least cost alternative can be determined using either the total-cost approach or the incremental approach. Exhibits 12-5 and 12-6 illustrate least-cost decisions.

H. Preference decisions involve ranking investment projects. Such a ranking is necessary whenever funds available for investment are limited.

1. Preference decisions are sometimes called *ranking* decisions or *rationing* decisions because they ration limited investment funds among competing investment opportunities.

2. The net present value of one project should not be compared directly to the net present value of another project, unless the investments in the projects are equal.

a. To make a valid comparison between projects that require different investments, a *project profitability index* is computed. The formula for the index is:

$$\text{Project profitability index} = \frac{\text{Net present value of the project}}{\text{Investment required}}$$

This is basically an application of the idea from Chapter 11 of utilization of a scarce resource. In this case, the scarce resource is the investment funds. The project profitability index is similar to the contribution margin per unit of the scarce resource.

b. The preference rule when using the project profitability index is: *The higher the project profitability index, the more desirable the project.*

H. Two other capital budgeting methods are considered in the chapter. These methods do not involve discounting cash flows One of these is the payback method.

1. The *payback method* focuses on how long it takes for a project to recover its initial cost out of the cash receipts it generates. The payback period is expressed in years.

a. When the cash inflows from the project are the same every year, the following formula can be used to compute the payback period:

$$\text{Payback period} = \frac{\text{Investment required}}{\text{Net annual cash inflows}}$$

b. If new equipment is replacing old equipment, the "investment required" should be reduced by any salvage value obtained from the disposal of old equipment. And in this case, in computing the "net annual cash inflows," only the incremental cash inflow provided by the new equipment over the old equipment should be used.

2. The payback period is not a measure of profitability. Rather it is a measure of how long it takes for a project to recover its investment cost.

3. The payback method ignores the time value of money and that ignores all cash flows that occur once the initial cost has been recovered. Therefore, this method is very crude and should be used only with a great deal of caution. Nevertheless, the payback method can be useful in industries where project lives are very short and uncertain.

I. The simple rate of return method is another capital budgeting method that does not involve discounted cash flows.

1. The *simple rate of return* method focuses on accounting net operating income, rather than on cash flows. The formula for its computation is:

$$\text{Simple rate of retun} = \frac{\text{Annual incremental net operating income}}{\text{Initial investment}}$$

If new equipment is replacing old equipment, then the "initial investment" in the new equipment is the cost of the new equipment reduced by any salvage value obtained from the old equipment.

2. Like the payback method, the simple rate of return method does not consider the time value of money. Therefore, the rate of return computed by this method will not be an accurate guide to the profitability of an investment project.

Appendix 12A: The Concept of Present Value

A. It is important to recognize the time value of money in capital budgeting analysis. A dollar received today is more valuable than a dollar received in the future for the simple reason that a dollar received today can be invested—yielding more than a dollar in the future.

B. Present value analysis recognizes the time value of money in capital budgeting decisions.

    1. Present value analysis involves expressing a future cash flow in terms of present dollars. When a future cash flow is expressed in terms of its present value, the process is called *discounting*.

    2. Use Table 12B-3 in Appendix 12B to determine the present value of a single sum to be received in the future. This table contains factors for various rates of interest for various periods, which when multiplied by a future sum, will give the sum's present value.

    3. Use Table 12B-4 in Appendix 12B to determine the present value of an *annuity*, or stream, of cash flows. This table contains factors that, when multiplied by the stream of cash flows, will give the stream's present value. Be careful to note that this annuity table is for a very specific type of annuity in which the first payment occurs at the end of the first year.

REVIEW AND SELF-TEST
Questions and Exercises

True or False

Enter a T or an F in the blank to indicate whether the statement is true or false.

____ 1. Under the net present value method, the present value of all cash inflows associated with an investment project is compared to the present value of all cash outflows, with the difference, or net present value, determining whether or not the project is acceptable.

____ 2. Cash outlays for noncurrent assets such as machines would be considered in a capital budgeting analysis, but not cash outlays for current assets such as inventory.

____ 3. The internal rate of return is the discount rate for which a project's net present value is zero.

____ 4. In present value analysis, the higher the discount rate, the higher is the present value of a given future cash inflow.

____ 5. When comparing two investment alternatives, the total-cost approach provides the same ultimate answer as the incremental-cost approach.

____ 6. In ranking investment projects, a project with a high net present value should be ranked above a project with a lower net present value.

____ 7. The simple rate of return method explicitly takes depreciation into account.

____ 8. The payback method does not consider the time value of money.

____ 9. The present value of a cash inflow to be received in 5 years is greater than the present value of the same sum to be received in 10 years.

Multiple Choice

Choose the best answer or response by placing the identifying letter in the space provided.

The following data relate to questions 1 and 2.

Peters Company is considering the purchase of a machine to further automate its production line. The machine would cost $30,000, and have a ten-year life with no salvage value. It would save $8,000 per year in labor costs, but would increase power costs by $1,000 annually. The company's discount rate is 12%.

____ 1. The present value of the net annual cost savings would be: a) $39,550; b) $45,200; c) $5,650; d) $70,000.

____ 2. The net present value of the proposed machine would be: a) $(15,200); b) $5,650; c) $9,550; d) $30,000.

____ 3. White Company's required rate of return and discount rate is 12%. The company is considering an investment opportunity that would yield a return of $10,000 in five years. What is the most that the company should be willing to invest in this project? a) $36,050; b) $5,670; c) $17,637; d) $2,774.

____ 4. Dover Company is considering an investment project in which a working capital investment of $30,000 would be required. The investment would provide cash inflows of $10,000 per year for six years. If the company's discount rate is 18%, and if the working capital is released at the end of the project, then the project's net present value is: a) $4,980; b) $(4,980); c) $16,080; d) $(12,360).

____ 5. Frumer Company has purchased a machine that cost $30,000, that will save $6,000 per year in cash operating costs, and that has an expected life of 15 years with zero salvage value. The payback period on the machine will be: a) 2 years; b) 7.5 years; c) 5 years; d) 0.2 years.

____ 6. Refer to the data in question (5) above. The simple rate of return on the machine is closest to: a) 20%; b) 13.3%; c) 18%; d) 10%.

Exercises

12-1. You have recently won $100,000 in a contest. You have been given the option of receiving $100,000 to-day or receiving $12,000 at the end of each year for the next 20 years.

a.   If you can earn 8% on investments, which of these two options would you select? (Note: The net present value method assumes that any cash flows are reinvested at a rate of return equal to the discount rate. Therefore, to answer this question you can compare the net present values of the cash flows under the two alternatives using 8% as the discount rate.)

Item	Year(s)	Amount of Cash Flows	8% Factor	Present Value of Cash Flows
Receive the annuity	_____	_____	_____	$_____
Receive the lump sum	_____	_____	_____	
Net present value in favor				_____
of _____ ..				$_____

b.   If you can earn 12% on investments, which of these two options would you select?

Item	Year(s)	Amount of Cash Flows	12% Factor	Present Value of Cash Flows
Receive the annuity	_____	$ _____	_____	$_____
Receive the lump sum	_____	_____	_____	
Net present value in favor				_____
of _____ ..				$_____

12-2. Lynde Company has been offered a contract to provide a key replacement part for the Army's main attack helicopter. The contract would expire in eight years. The projected cash flows that result from the contract are given below:

Cost of new equipment	$300,000
Working capital needed	100,000
Net annual cash inflows	85,000
Salvage value of equipment in eight years	50,000

The company's required rate of return and discount rate is 16%. The working capital would be released for use elsewhere at the end of the project.

Complete the analysis below to determine whether the contract should be accepted.

Item	Year(s)	Amount of Cash Flows	16% Factor	Present Value of Cash Flows
Cost of new equipment	_____	$ _____	_____	$ _____
Working capital needed	_____	_____	_____	_____
Net annual cash inflows	_____	_____	_____	_____
Salvage value of equipment	_____	_____	_____	_____
Working capital released	_____	_____	_____	_____
Salvage value of equipment	_____	_____	_____	_____
Net present value				$ _____

Should the contract be accepted? Explain.

_____

_____

_____

_____

_____

_____

_____

12-3. Harlan Company would like to purchase a new machine that makes wonderfully smooth fruit sorbet that the company can sell in the premium frozen dessert sections of supermarkets. The machine costs $450,000 and has a useful life of ten years with a salvage value of $50,000. Annual revenues and expenses resulting from the new machine are:

Sales revenue..		$300,000
Less selling and administrative expenses:		
Advertising	$100,000	
Salaries of operators.......................	70,000	
Maintenance...................................	30,000	
Depreciation..................................	40,000	240,000
Net operating income		$ 60,000

a. Harlan Company will not invest in new equipment unless it promises a payback period of 4 years or less. Compute the payback period on the sorbet machine.

Computation of the net annual cash inflow:

Net operating income .... $ _____

Add: Noncash deduction for depreciation .... _____

Net annual cash inflow .... $ _____

Computation of the payback period:

$$\text{Payback period} = \frac{\text{Investment required}}{\text{Net annual cash inflows}}$$

$$= \frac{\overline{}}{} = \_\_\_\_\_ \text{ years}$$

b. Compute the simple rate of return on the investment in the new machine.

$$\frac{\text{Simple rate}}{\text{of retun}} = \frac{\text{Annual incremental net operating income}}{\text{Initial investment}}$$

$$= \frac{\overline{}}{} = \_\_\_\_$$

Answers to Questions and Exercises

True or False

1. **T** Exhibit 12-2 illustrates this point.

2. **F** All cash flows should be included in a capital budgeting analysis.

3. **T** This statement is true by definition.

4. **F** The opposite is true—the higher the discount rate, the lower the present value of a given future cash inflow.

5. **T** The total-cost approach and the incremental-cost approach are just different ways of obtaining the same result.

6. **F** Net present value shouldn't be used to rank projects when investment funds are limited, since one project may have a higher net present value than another simply because it is larger. The project profitability index should be used to compare projects in this situation.

7. **T** This point is illustrated in formulas (3) and (4) in the text.

8. **T** A major defect of the payback method is that dollars are given the same weight regardless of when they are received.

9. **T** When discounting the shorter the time period, the greater the present value.

Multiple Choice

1. **a** The computations are:

Savings in labor costs	$ 8,000
Less increased power costs	1,000
Net cost savings	$ 7,000
Present value factor for 12% for 10 years (Table 12B-4)	× 5.650
Present value of cost savings	$39,550

2. **c** The computations are:

Investment in the machine	$(30,000)
Present value of cost savings	39,550
Net present value	$ 9,550

3. **b** The computations are:

Return in 5 years	$10,000
Factor for 12% for 5 years (Table 12B-3)	× 0.567
Present value	$ 5,670

   This is the maximum amount the company is willing to invest. If it were to invest more than $5,670, the net present value of the investment would be negative.

4. **c** The computations are:

	Year(s)	Amount	18% Factor	Present Value
Working capital investment	Now	$(30,000)	1.000	$(30,000)
Cash inflow	1-6	10,000	3.498	34,980
Working capital released	6	30,000	0.370	11,100
Net present value				$ 16,080

5. **c** The computation is:

   $$\frac{\text{Payback}}{\text{period}} = \frac{\text{Investment required}}{\text{Net annual cash inflows}}$$

   $$= \frac{\$30,000}{\$6,000 \text{ per year}} = 5 \text{ years}$$

6. **b** The computation is:

   $$\frac{\text{Simple rate}}{\text{of return}} = \frac{\text{Annual incremental net operating income}}{\text{Initial investment}}$$

   $$= \frac{\$6,000 - \$2,000}{\$30,000} = 13.1\%$$

   The incremental revenue is the cost savings of $6,000 per year.
   The incremental expense is the annual depreciation charge of $2,000 = $30,000 ÷ 15 years.

Exercises

12-1. a. The annuity is preferable if the discount rate is 8%:

Item	Year(s)	Amount of Cash Flows	8% Factor	Present Value of Cash Flows
Receive the annuity	1-20	$ 12,000	9.818	$117,816
Receive the lump sum	Now	100,000	1.000	100,000
Net present value in favor of the annuity				$ 17,816

   b. The lump sum is preferable if the discount rate is 12%:

Item	Year(s)	Amount of Cash Flows	12% Factor	Present Value of Cash Flows
Receive the annuity	1-20	$ 12,000	7.469	$ 89,628
Receive the lump sum	Now	100,000	1.000	100,000
Net present value in favor of the lump sum				$ 10,372

12-2.

Item	Year(s)	Amount of Cash Flows	16% Factor	Present Value of Cash Flows
Cost of new equipment	Now	($300,000)	1.000	($300,000)
Working capital needed	Now	(100,000)	1.000	(100,000)
Net annual cash receipts	1-8	85,000	4.344	369,240
Salvage value of equipment	8	50,000	0.305	15,250
Working capital released	8	100,000	0.305	30,500
Net present value				$ 14,990

   Yes, the contract should be accepted. The net present value is positive, which means that the contract will provide more than the company's 16% required rate of return.

12-3. a. The net annual cash inflow would be:

Net operating income	$ 60,000
Add: Noncash deduction for depreciation	40,000
Net annual cash inflow	$100,000

   The payback period would be:

$$\text{Payback period} = \frac{\text{Investment required}}{\text{Net annual cash inflows}} = \frac{\$450,000}{\$100,000 \text{ per year}} = 4.5 \text{ years}$$

   The machine would not be purchased since it will not provide the 4-year payback period required by the company.

   b. The simple rate of return would be:

$$\text{Simple rate of return} = \frac{\text{Annual incremental net operating income}}{\text{Initial investment}}$$

$$= \frac{\$60,000}{\$450,000} = 13.3\%$$

Chapter 13

"How Well Am I Doing?"— Statement of Cash Flows

Chapter Study Suggestions

This chapter explains how to prepare a statement of cash flows. The statement of cash flows is constructed by examining changes in balance sheet accounts. The chapter contains three key exhibits. The first, Exhibit 13-2, classifies changes in balance sheet accounts as sources and uses of cash. The second key exhibit is Exhibit 13-7, which provides guidelines for classifying transactions as operating, investing, and financing activities. Once transactions have been classified as sources or uses and as operating, investing, or financing activities, it is fairly straightforward to put together a statement of cash flows. However, you must keep track of many details. Therefore, we recommend a systematic approach based on a worksheet such as the one in Exhibit 13-9 or the T-account approach in Appendix 13B.

CHAPTER HIGHLIGHTS

A.   The purpose of the statement of cash flows is to highlight the major activities that have provided and used cash during the period.

B.   The term *cash* on the statement of cash flows is broadly defined to include both cash and cash equivalents. Cash equivalents consist of short-term, highly liquid investments such as treasury bills, commercial paper, and money market funds that are made solely for the purpose of generating a return on temporarily idle funds.

C.   A period's net cash flow is equal to the change in the cash account during the period. Exhibit 13-1 shows that the change in cash during a period can be expressed in terms of the changes in all of the noncash balance sheet accounts. The statement of cash flows is based on this fact. The statement of cash flows is basically a listing of changes in the noncash balance sheet accounts.

D.   Changes in noncash account balances can be classified as *sources* and *uses*. On the statement of cash flows, sources positively affect cash flow and uses negatively affect cash flow.

   1.   The following are classified as sources:
      a.   Net operating income.
      b.   Decreases in noncash assets.
      c.   Increases in liabilities.
      d.   Increases in capital stock accounts.

   2.   The following are classified as uses:
      a.   Increases in noncash assets.
      b.   Decreases in liabilities.
      c.   Decreases in capital stock accounts.
      d.   Dividends paid to shareholders.

   3.   The sources and uses are usually intuitive. For example, an increase in inventory (a noncash asset) implicitly requires cash and is considered to be a use.

E.   The FASB requires that the statement of cash flows be divided into three sections. These sections relate to *operating activities, investing activities, and financing activities.*

   1.   As a general rule, operating activities enter directly or indirectly into the determination of net operating income. These activities include:

      a.   Net operating income (or net loss).

      b.   Changes in current assets.

      c.   Changes in noncurrent assets that affect net operating income, such as depreciation and amortization.

      d.   Changes in current liabilities (except for debts to lenders and dividends).

      e.   Changes in noncurrent liabilities that affect net income, such as interest on debt.

   2.   Investing activities consist of changes in noncurrent assets that are not included in net income.

   3.   Financing activities consist of transactions involving borrowing from creditors (other than the payment of interest), and transactions involving the owners of a company. Specific financing activities include:

      a.   Changes in current liabilities that are debts to lenders rather than obligations to suppliers, employees, or government.

      b.   Changes in noncurrent liabilities that are not included in net income.

      c.   Changes in capital stock accounts.

      d.   Dividends paid to the company's shareholders.

F.   In some cases, the net change in an account is shown on the statement of cash flows. In other cases, the increases and decreases are disclosed separately. The treatment depends on whether the change appears in the operating activities section or in the investing and financing activities sections.

   1.   For both financing and investing activities, items on the statement of cash flows must be presented in gross amounts rather than in net amounts. For example, if a company buys $100,000 of new equipment and sells $30,000 of used equipment, both amounts must be disclosed rather than the net effect of a $70,000 increase in the equipment account.

   2.   For operating activities, only the net change in an account is shown on the statement of cash flows.

G.   The net result of the cash inflows and outflows arising from operating activities is referred to as the *net cash provided by operating activities.* This figure can be computed using the *direct method* or the *indirect method.*

   1.   Under the direct method, the income statement is reconstructed on a cash basis from top to bottom. This method is discussed in Appendix 13A.

   2.   Under the indirect method, the net cash provided by operations is computed by starting with net income and adjusting it to a cash basis. The steps to follow in this adjustment process are shown in Exhibit 13-8.

3. The direct and indirect methods yield exactly the same figure for the net cash provided by operating activities.

H. Carefully study Exhibit 13-9, which illustrates the mechanics of using a worksheet to construct the statement of cash flows. Make sure you understand each of the entries on this worksheet.

I. Carefully study Exhibit 13-11, which illustrates the format of the statement of cash flows. Trace each of the entries from the worksheet in Exhibit 13-9 to the statement of cash flows in Exhibit 13-11.

Appendix 13A: The Direct Method

A. The direct method differs from the indirect method only in the operating activities section of the statement of cash flows. The investing and financing activities sections of the statement are identical for the direct and indirect methods.

B. In the indirect method, the income statement is reconstructed from the top down by converting it to a cash basis.

    1. To adjust revenue to a cash basis:
- Subtract (add) any increase (decrease) in accounts receivable.

    2. To adjust cost of goods sold to a cash basis:
- Add (subtract) any increase (decrease) in inventory.
- Subtract (add) any increase (decrease) in accounts payable.

3. To adjust operating expenses to a cash basis:
- Add (subtract) any increase (decrease) in prepaid expenses.
- Subtract (add) any increase (decrease) in accrued liabilities.
- Subtract the period's depreciation and amortization charges.

4. To adjust income tax expense to a cash basis:
- Subtract (add) any increase (decrease) in taxes payable.
- Subtract (add) any increase (decrease) in deferred taxes.

Appendix 13B: The T-account Approach

A. T-accounts can be used can be used instead of a worksheet to prepare the statement of cash flows.

B. To use the T-account approach, create a blank T-account for cash and T-accounts for each noncash balance sheet account. Enter the beginning and ending balances in the noncash T-accounts. Then analyze each of the noncash T-accounts, making entries much like journal entries to reconcile the beginning and ending balances. Decreases in assets, increases in liabilities, and increases in stockholders' equity accounts are offset by debits to the cash T-account. Increases in assets, decreases in liabilities, and decreases in stockholders' equity accounts are offset by credits to the cash T-account.

C. When the beginning and ending balances in all of the noncash balance sheet accounts have been reconciled, all of the data for constructing the statement of cash flows will be in the cash T-account.

REVIEW AND SELF-TEST
Questions and Exercises

True or False

Enter a T or an F in the blank to indicate whether the statement is true or false.

____ 1. Dividends received on stock held as an investment are included in the operating activities section of the statement of cash flows.

____ 2. Interest paid on amounts borrowed is included in the financing activities section of the statement of cash flows.

____ 3. Lending money to another entity (such as to a subsidiary) is classified as a financing activity.

____ 4. Paying cash dividends to the company's stockholders is classified as a financing activity.

____ 5. Transactions involving all forms of debt—including accounts payable, short-term borrowing, and long-term borrowing—are classified as financing activities on the statement of cash flows.

____ 6. For both financing and investing activities, items on the statement of cash flows should be presented gross rather than net.

____ 7. The direct and indirect methods can yield different amounts for the net cash provided by operating activities.

____ 8. Only changes in noncurrent accounts are analyzed for a statement of cash flows.

____ 9. If a company is profitable, the net cash flow must be positive.

____ 10. (Appendix 13A) The income statement is reconstructed on a cash basis from top to bottom under the direct method of computing the net cash provided by operating activities.

____ 11. (Appendix 13A) In computing the net cash provided by operating activities, depreciation is added to net income under the indirect method, but it is deducted from operating expenses under the direct method.

Multiple Choice

Choose the best answer or response by placing the identifying letter in the space provided.

____ 1. For purposes of constructing a statement of cash flows, an increase in inventory would be classified as: a) a source and an operating activity; b) a use and an operating activity; c) a source and an investing activity; d) a use and an investing activity.

____ 2. An increase in accounts payable would be classified as: a) a source and an operating activity; b) a use and an operating activity; c) a source and a financing activity; d) a use and a financing activity.

____ 3. An increase in bonds payable would be classified as: a) a source and an investing activity; b) a use and an investing activity; c) a source and a financing activity; d) a use and a financing activity.

____ 4. An increase in long-term investments would be classified as: a) a source and an investing activity; b) a use and an investing activity; c) a source and a financing activity; d) a use and a financing activity.

____ 5. Cash dividends paid to the company's stockholders would be classified as: a) a source and an operating activity; b) a use and an operating activity; c) a source and a financing activity; d) a use and a financing activity.

____ 6. An increase in the company's common stock account would be classified as: a) a source and an investing activity; b) a use and an investing activity; c) a source and a financing activity; d) a use and a financing activity.

Exercises

13-1. Ingall Company's comparative balance sheet and income statement for the most recent year follow:

Ingall Company
Comparative Balance Sheet
(dollars in millions)

	Ending Balance	Beginning Balance
Assets		
Cash	$ 14	$ 10
Accounts receivable	21	15
Inventory	50	43
Prepaid expenses	2	6
Plant and equipment	190	140
Less accumulated depreciation	(65)	(54)
Long-term investments	70	90
Total assets	$282	$250
Liabilities and Stockholders' Equity		
Accounts payable	$ 26	$ 25
Accrued liabilities	10	12
Taxes payable	13	18
Bonds payable	50	40
Deferred income taxes	36	31
Common stock	80	70
Retained earnings	67	54
Total liabilities and stockholders' equity	$282	$250

Ingall Company
Income Statement
(dollars in millions)

Sales	$230
Cost of goods sold	120
Gross margin	110
Operating expenses	70
Net operating income	40
Gain on sale of long-term investments	5
Income before taxes	45
Income taxes	14
Net income	$ 31

Notes: Dividends of $18 million were declared and paid during the year. The gain on sale of long-term investments was from the sale of investments for $25 million in cash. These investments had an original cost of $20 million. There were no retirements or disposals of plant or equipment during the year.

Using the blank form on the following page, prepare a worksheet like Exhibit 13-10 for Ingall Company.

Ingall Company
Statement of Cash Flows Worksheet

	Change	Source or use?	Cash Flow Effect	Adjust-ments	Adjusted Effect	Classi-fication
Assets (except cash and cash equivalents)						
Current assets:						
Accounts receivable............................	___	___	___		___	___
Inventory..	___	___	___		___	___
Prepaid expenses................................	___	___	___		___	___
Noncurrent assets:						
Plant and equipment	___	___	___		___	___
Long-term investments	___	___	___	___	___	___
Liabilities, Contra-Assets, and Stockholders' Equity						
Contra-assets:						
Accumulated depreciation	___	___	___		___	
Current liabilities:						
Accounts payable..............................	___	___	___		___	
Accrued liabilities.............................	___	___	___		___	
Taxes payable	___	___	___		___	
Noncurrent liabilities:						
Bonds payable	___	___	___		___	
Deferred income taxes	___	___	___		___	
Stockholders' equity:						
Common stock.................................	___	___	___		___	
Retained earnings						
Net income.....................................	___	___	___		___	
Dividends.......................................	___	___	___		___	
Additional Entries						
Proceeds from sale of						
long-term investments			___	___	___	
Gain on sale of long-term investments...			___	___	___	
Total (net cash flow)			___	___	___	

13-2. Determine Ingall Company's net cash provided by operating activities using the indirect method.

Net income .... $ _____

Adjustments to convert net income to a cash basis:

    Depreciation charges.. _____

    _____ in accounts receivable .... _____

    _____ in inventory .... _____

    _____ in prepaid expenses .... _____

    _____ in accounts payable .... _____

    _____ in accrued liabilities....................................... _____

    _____ in taxes payable .... _____

    _____ in deferred taxes .... _____

    Gain on sale of long-term investments................................... _____

Net cash flow provided by (used in) operations .... $ _____

13-3. (Appendix 13A) Using the direct method, determine Ingall Company's net cash provided by operating activities.

Sales .... $ 230

Adjustments to convert sales to a cash basis:

    _____ in accounts receivable.................................... _____ $ _____

Cost of goods sold... $ 120

Adjustments to convert cost of goods sold to a cash basis:

    _____ in inventory.. _____

    _____ in accounts payable.. _____   _____

Operating expenses.. $ 70

Adjustments to convert operating expenses to a cash basis:

    _____ in prepaid expenses.. _____

    _____ in accrued liabilities....................................... _____

    Depreciation charges .... _____   _____

Income taxes.. $ 14

Adjustments to convert income taxes to a cash basis:

    _____ in taxes payable .... _____

    _____ in deferred taxes .... _____   _____

Net cash provided by (used in) operating activities........................ $ _____

13-4.   Prepare a statement of cash flows for Ingall Company using the form below.

Ingall Company
Statement of Cash Flows

Operating activities

Net cash provided by (used in) operating activities....................................... $_____

Investing activities

_____ .... $_____

_____ ....   _____

Net cash provided by (used in) investing activities ....   _____

Financing activities

_____ .... $_____

_____ ....   _____

_____ ....   _____

Net cash provided by (used in) financing activities................................   _____

Net increase (decrease) in cash...   _____

Cash balance, beginning..   _____

Cash balance, ending .... $_____

13-5   (Appendix 13B) Using the data for Ingall Company in 13-1, fill in the following T-accounts.

Cash

	Provided	Used

Accounts Receivable		
Bal.	15	
Bal.	21	

Inventory		
Bal.	43	
Bal.	50	

Prepaid Expenses		
Bal.	6	
Bal.	2	

Plant and Equipment		
Bal.	140	
Bal.	190	

Accumulated Depreciation		
	54	Bal.
	65	Bal.

Long-Term Investments		
Bal.	90	
Bal.	70	

Accounts Payable		
	25	Bal.
	26	Bal.

Accrued Liabilities		
	12	Bal.
	10	Bal.

Taxes Payable		
	18	Bal.
	13	Bal.

Bonds Payable		
	40	Bal.
	50	Bal.

Deferred Income Taxes		
	31	Bal.
	36	Bal.

Common Stock		
	70	Bal.
	80	Bal.

Retained Earnings		
	54	Bal.
	67	Bal.

Answers to Questions and Exercises

True or False

1. T Dividends received are included in net income and therefore are included in operating rather than investing activities.

2. F Interest paid on amounts borrowed is included in operating activities since interest enters into net income.

3. F Lending money to another entity is classified as an investing activity.

4. T Dividends do not affect net income and therefore are not considered to be an operating activity.

5. F Transactions involving accounts payable are included among operating activities—not financing activities.

6. T Only transactions involving operating activities are presented in net amounts.

7. F The direct and indirect methods will always yield exactly the same amount for the net cash provided by operating activities.

8. F Changes in all noncash accounts, current as well as noncurrent, are analyzed when preparing a statement of cash flows.

9. F The net cash flow may be negative even if a company is profitable. For example, a profitable company may make a major investment using cash reserves it has accumulated in the past.

10. T See Exhibit 13A-1 for an example.

11. T Subtracting depreciation from an expense is equivalent to adding it to net income.

Multiple Choice

1. b Inventory is a current asset. Increases in current assets are classified as uses. Changes in current assets are considered to be the result of operating activities.

2. a Accounts payable is a current liability. Increases in current liabilities are classified as sources. Changes in current liabilities are considered to be the result of operating activities.

3. c Bonds payable is a noncurrent liability. An increase in a noncurrent liability is considered to be a source. A change in a noncurrent liability is considered to be a financing activity unless it enters into net income.

4. b Long-term investments is a noncurrent asset account. An increase in a noncurrent asset is considered to be a use. A change in a noncurrent asset is considered to be an investing activity unless it directly enters into the determination of net income.

5. d Dividends are considered to be a use. They are classified as a financing activity since they do not enter into the determination of net income.

6. c An increase in the common stock account is considered to be a source and a financing activity.

Exercises

13-1. The completed worksheet for Ingall Company appears below:

	Change	Source or use?	Cash Flow Effect	Adjust-ments	Adjusted Effect	Classi-fication*
Assets (except cash and cash equivalents)						
Current assets:						
Accounts receivable.....................	+6	Use	-6		-6	Operating
Inventory....................................	+7	Use	-7		-7	Operating
Prepaid expenses........................	-4	Source	+4		+4	Operating
Noncurrent assets:						
Plant and equipment	+50	Use	-50		-50	Investing
Long-term investments	-20	Source	+20	-20	0	Investing
Liabilities, Contra-Assets, and Stockholders' Equity						
Contra-assets:						
Accumulated depreciation	+11	Source	+11		+11	Operating
Current liabilities:						
Accounts payable........................	+1	Source	+1		+1	Operating
Accrued liabilities.......................	-2	Use	-2		-2	Operating
Taxes payable	-5	Use	-5		-5	Operating
Noncurrent liabilities:						
Bonds payable	+10	Source	+10		+10	Financing
Deferred income taxes	+5	Source	+5		+5	Operating
Stockholders' equity:						
Common stock............................	+10	Source	+10		+10	Financing
Retained earnings						
Net income................................	+31	Source	+31		+31	Operating
Dividends..................................	-18	Use	-18		-18	Financing
Additional Entries						
Proceeds from sale of						
long-term investments..................				+25	+25	Investing
Gain on sale of long-term						
investments.................................				-5	-5	Operating
Total (net cash flow)			+4	0	+4	

Note: The most difficult part of this worksheet is the adjustment for the sale of the long-term investments. Basically, the adjustment moves the gain on the sale from the operating activities section to the investing section. It would be wise to pay particular attention to this entry and how it affects the statement of cash flows.

13-2.   The operating activities section of the statement of cash flows constructed using the indirect method appears below:

Net income	$31
Adjustments to convert net income to a cash basis:	
Depreciation charges..	11
Increase in accounts receivable...	(6)
Increase in inventory..	(7)
Decrease in prepaid expenses..	4
Increase in accounts payable...	1
Decrease in accrued liabilities...	(2)
Decrease in taxes payable	(5)
Increase in deferred taxes..	5
Gain on sale of long-term investments....................................	(5)
Net cash flow provided by operations	$27

Note that the gain on sale of long-term investments is deducted from net income. This removes the gain from the operating activities section of the statement of cash flows. The gain will show up implicitly in the investing activities section of the statement of cash flows. See the solution to 13-4 below.

13-3.   The direct method can be used to arrive at the same answer as in 13-2 above.

Sales	$230	
Adjustments to convert sales to a cash basis:		
Increase in accounts receivable	(6)	$224
Cost of goods sold...	120	
Adjustments to convert cost of goods sold to a cash basis:		
Increase in inventory	7	
Increase in accounts payable	(1)	126
Operating expenses	70	
Adjustments to convert operating expenses to a cash basis:		
Decrease in prepaid expenses...	(4)	
Decrease in accrued liabilities	2	
Depreciation charges	(11)	57
Income taxes..	14	
Adjustments to convert income taxes to a cash basis:		
Decrease in taxes payable	5	
Increase in deferred taxes..	(5)	14
Net cash provided by operating activities...		$ 27

13-4.

Ingall Company
Statement of Cash Flows

Operating activities
Net cash provided by operating activities .... $ 27

Investing activities
    Proceeds from sale of long-term investments $25
    Increase in plant and equipment.. (50)
Net cash used for investing activities .... (25)

Financing activities
    Increase in bonds payable 10
    Increase in common stock.. 10
    Dividends .... (18)
Net cash provided by financing activities 2

Net increase in cash... 4
Cash balance, beginning.. 10
Cash balance, ending.. $14

13-5

		Cash			
		Provided	Used		
Net income	(1)	31	6	(3)	Increase in accounts receivable
Decrease in prepaid expenses	(5)	4	7	(4)	Increase in inventory
Increase in accumulated depreciation	(7)	11	5	(8)	Gain on sale of long-term investments
Increase in accounts payable	(9)	1	2	(10)	Decrease in accrued liabilities
Increase in deferred taxes	(13)	5	5	(11)	Decrease in taxes payable
Net cash provided by operating activities		27			
Proceeds from sale of long-term investments	(8)	25	50	(6)	Increase in plant and equipment
Net cash used for investing activities			25		
Increase in bonds payable	(12)	10	18	(2)	Cash dividends paid
Increase in common stock	(14)	10			
Net cash provided by financing activities		2			
Net increase in cash		4			

Accounts Receivable			Inventory			Prepaid Expenses		
Bal.	15		Bal.	43		Bal.	6	
(3)	6		(4)	7			4	(5)
Bal.	21		Bal.	50		Bal.	2	

	Plant and Equipment	
Bal.	140	
(6)	50	
Bal.	190	

	Accumulated Depreciation	
		54 Bal.
		11 (7)
		65 Bal.

	Long-Term Investments	
Bal.	90	
		20 (8)
Bal.	70	

	Accounts Payable	
		25 Bal.
		1 (9)
		26 Bal.

	Accrued Liabilities	
(10)	2	12 Bal.
		10 Bal.

	Taxes Payable	
(11)	5	18 Bal.
		13 Bal.

	Bonds Payable	
		40 Bal.
		10 (12)
		50 Bal.

	Deferred Income Taxes	
		31 Bal.
		5 (13)
		36 Bal.

	Common Stock	
		70 Bal.
		10 (14)
		80 Bal.

	Retained Earnings	
		54 Bal.
(2)	18	31 (1)
		67 Bal.

Note: The gain on the sale of long-term investments would be entered as follows:

(8)

Proceeds from Sale of Long-Term Investments	25	
Long-Term Investments		20
Gain on Sale		5

Chapter 14

"How Well Am I Doing?"—
Financial Statement Analysis

Chapter Study Suggestions

The chapter is divided into two parts. The first part discusses the preparation and use of statements in comparative and common-size form. This part of the chapter is easy and involves nothing more complicated than computing percentages. Your study in this part should be focused on Exhibits 14-1, 14-2, and 14-4 in the text. These exhibits show how statements in comparative and common-size form are prepared.

The second part of the chapter deals with ratio analysis. Altogether, seventeen ratios are presented in this part of the chapter. You should memorize the formula for each ratio since it is likely that you will be expected to know these formulas on exams. This may at first seem like an overwhelming task, but most of the ratios are intuitive and easy to compute. You should also learn how to interpret each ratio. Exhibit 14-7 in the text provides a compact summary of the ratios.

CHAPTER HIGHLIGHTS

A.   Financial statement analysis is concerned with assessing the financial condition of a company. To be most useful, comparisons should be made from one year to another, as well as with other companies within the same industry.

B.   Three common analytical techniques for financial statement analysis are: 1) dollar and percentage changes on statements (horizontal analysis); 2) common-size statements (vertical analysis); and 3) ratios.

   1.   In horizontal analysis two or more yearly statements are placed side by side and changes between years are analyzed. These comparisons are made both in terms of dollars and percentage changes from year to year.

      a.   Showing changes in dollar form helps to identify the most significant changes.

      b.   Showing changes in percentage form helps to identify the most unusual changes.

      c.   In trend percentage analysis, each item, such as sales or net income, is stated as a percentage of the same item in a base year.

   2.   In a common-size statement, amounts on the balance sheet are stated as a percentage of total assets and amounts on the income statement are stated as a percentage of sales. Showing the balance sheet and the income statement in common-size form helps to highlight the relative importance of the various items. Preparation of common-size statements is known as vertical analysis.

   3.   The *gross margin percentage* is a particularly important item on the common-size income statement. It is defined as follows:

$$\text{Gross margin percentage} = \frac{\text{Gross margin}}{\text{Sales}}$$

The gross margin percentage is a rough measure of the overall profitability of a company's products. In manufacturing companies, the gross margin percentage should increase as sales increase since fixed manufacturing costs are spread across more units.

   4.   In addition to horizontal and vertical analysis, stockholders, short-term creditors, and long-term creditors use a variety of ratios to help them evaluate companies. Ratios that are designed to meet the needs of these three different groups are discussed in sections C, D, and E below.

C.   Several ratios provide measures of how well the company is doing from the shareholders' perspective.

   1.   *Earnings per share* is defined as follows:

$$\frac{\text{Earnings}}{\text{per share}} = \frac{\text{Net income-Preferred dividends}}{\text{Average number of common shares outstanding}}$$

Preferred dividends are subtracted from net income since they are not an expense on the income statement but reduce the earnings that can be distributed to common shareholders.

   2.   The *price-earnings ratio* shows the relation between the market price of a share of stock and the stock's current earnings per share. The price-earnings ratio is computed as follows:

$$\text{Price-earnings ratio} = \frac{\text{Market price per share}}{\text{Earnings per share}}$$

Price-earnings ratios tend to be similar for companies in the same industry. One of the biggest factors affecting the price-earnings ratio is future earnings growth. If investors believe one company is likely to have higher future earnings growth than another, they will bid up the price of the stock with a higher expected future earnings growth and hence it will have a high price-earnings ratio.

   3.   The *dividend payout ratio* measures the proportion of current earnings being paid out as dividends. The formula is:

$$\text{Dividend payout ratio} = \frac{\text{Dividends per share}}{\text{Earnings per share}}$$

A company with a high dividend payout ratio is paying out most of its earnings to shareholders as dividends rather than reinvesting the earnings in the company.

   4.   The *dividend yield ratio* measures the cash yield on the common stockholder's investment. The ratio is computed as follows:

$$\text{Dividend yield ratio} = \frac{\text{Dividends per share}}{\text{Market price per share}}$$

Investors hope to profit from both dividends and increases in the market value of the stock they own. The dividend yield measures only the contribution of the dividends. Note that the current market price per share is used in this ratio and not the price the investor originally paid for the shares.

   5.   The *return on total assets* is a measure of how effectively a company has used its assets. The formula is:

$$\text{Return on total assets} = \frac{\text{Net income} + \left[\begin{array}{c}\text{Interest expense} \times \\ (1\text{-Tax rate})\end{array}\right]}{\text{Average total assets}}$$

a.   Note that interest expense is placed on an after-tax basis by multiplying it by one minus the tax rate before being added back to net income.

b.   Interest expense is added back to net income to show earnings *before* any distributions have been made to creditors and shareholders. This adjustment results in a total return on assets that measures operating performance independently of how the assets were financed.

6.   The *return on common stockholders' equity* measures a company's ability to generate income. The formula is:

$$\text{Return on common stockholders' equity} = \frac{\text{Net income} - \text{Preferred dividends}}{\text{Average common stockholders' equity}}$$

As with earnings per share, preferred dividends are subtracted from net income since preferred dividends reduce the earnings available to common shareholders. The return on common stockholders' equity is often higher than the return on total assets because of financial leverage.

a.   *Financial leverage* involves purchasing assets with funds obtained from creditors. If the assets in which the funds are invested earn a greater return than the rate of return required by creditors, then financial leverage is *positive*. Financial leverage is *negative* if the assets earn a return that is less than the rate of return required by creditors.

b.   Sources of leverage include long-term debt, preferred stock, and current liabilities.

c.   Long-term debt is usually a more effective source of financial leverage than preferred stock since interest on long-term debt is tax-deductible, whereas dividends on preferred stock are not.

7.   The *book value per share* measures the common stockholders' equity on a per share basis. The formula is:

$$\text{Book value per share} = \frac{\text{Common stockholders' equity}}{\text{Number of common shares outstanding}}$$

a.   Note that the denominator in this ratio is the number of common shares outstanding at the end of the year—not the average number of shares outstanding over the year as in the earnings per share calculation.

b.   Book value per share is usually less than market value per share. Market value reflects investors' expectations concerning future earnings and dividends. By contrast, book value measures financial effects of already completed transactions and hence looks to the past. Because of this, book value is of limited usefulness.

D.   Short-term creditors are concerned with being paid on time and are far more concerned with a company's financial assets and cash flows than with its accounting net income.

1.   *Working capital* measures the excess of current assets over current liabilities.

$$\text{Working capital} = \text{Current assets} - \text{Current liabilities}$$

Negative working capital signals that current assets are insufficient to cover current liabilities.

2.   The *current ratio* is also a widely used measure of short-term debt-paying ability. The formula is:

$$\text{Current ratio} = \frac{\text{Current assets}}{\text{Current liabilities}}$$

The current ratio, as well as working capital, should be interpreted with care. The *composition* of the assets and liabilities is very important. A high current ratio does not necessarily mean that the company is easily able to pay its current liabilities. For example, most of the current assets may be inventory that is difficult to sell quickly.

3.   The *acid-test* or *quick ratio* is designed to measure how well a company can meet its short-term obligations using only its *most liquid* current assets. The formula is:

$$\text{Acid-test ratio} = \frac{\begin{array}{c}\text{Cash} + \text{Marketable securities} \\ + \text{Current receivables}\end{array}}{\text{Current liabilities}}$$

Current receivables includes accounts receivable and short-term notes receivable. The current assets in this ratio do not include inventories or prepaid assets since they may be difficult to convert into cash.

4.   The *accounts receivable turnover* ratio measures the relation between sales on account and accounts receivable. The formula is:

$$\text{Accounts receivable turnover} = \frac{\text{Sales on account}}{\begin{array}{c}\text{Average accounts} \\ \text{receivable balance}\end{array}}$$

The higher this ratio, the quicker accounts receivable are collected. This is easier to see if the accounts receivable turnover is divided into 365 days. This gives the *average collection period*, which is computed as follows:

$$\text{Average collection period} = \frac{365 \text{ days}}{\text{Accounts receivable turnover}}$$

As its name implies, the average collection period indicates the average number of days required to collect credit sales. Ordinarily a short average collection period is desirable.

5. The *inventory turnover* ratio relates cost of goods sold to the average inventory balance using the following formula:

$$\text{Inventory turnover} = \frac{\text{Cost of goods sold}}{\text{Average inventory balance}}$$

The higher this ratio, the quicker inventory is sold. The *average sale period* measures how many days on average it takes to sell inventory. The formula is:

$$\text{Average sale period} = \frac{365 \text{ days}}{\text{Inventory turnover}}$$

The average sale period can differ dramatically from one industry to another. For example, the average sale period is much shorter in a florist shop than in a jewelry shop. Florists have to sell their inventory quickly or it will perish.

E. Long-term creditors are concerned with both the near-term and the long-term ability of a company to repay its debts.

1. The *times interest earned ratio* measures the ability of a company to pay the interest it owes. The formula is:

$$\text{Times interest earned} = \frac{\text{Earnings before interest expense and income taxes}}{\text{Interest expense}}$$

Generally, the higher the times interest earned, the greater the ability of the company to make interest payments.

2. The *debt-to-equity ratio* relates debt to equity using the following formula:

$$\text{Debt-to-equity ratio} = \frac{\text{Total liabilities}}{\text{Stockholders' equity}}$$

The lower this ratio, the greater the excess of assets over liabilities. Therefore creditors generally prefer a low debt-to-equity ratio since this provides a large cushion of protection.

REVIEW AND SELF-TEST
Questions and Exercises

True or False

Enter a T or an F in the blank to indicate whether the statement is true or false.

____ 1. Horizontal analysis uses dollar and percentage changes from year to year to highlight trends.

____ 2. Common-size statements focus on companies of similar size and operations.

____ 3. The current ratio is current assets less current liabilities.

____ 4. Trend percentages in financial statements would be an example of vertical analysis.

____ 5. A common-size statement shows items in percentage form, with each item stated as a percentage of a total of which that item is a part.

____ 6. Earnings per share is computed after deducting preferred dividends from the net income of a company.

____ 7. If earnings remain unchanged and the price-earnings ratio goes up, then the market price of the stock must have gone down.

____ 8. Dividing the market price of a share of stock by the dividends per share gives the price-earnings ratio.

____ 9. Book value per share is not a good predictor of future earnings potential.

____ 10. The acid test ratio excludes inventories from current assets.

____ 11. When computing the return on total assets, after-tax interest expense is subtracted from net income.

____ 12. Inventory turnover is computed by dividing sales by average inventory.

____ 13. If a company's return on total assets is substantially higher than its cost of borrowing, then the common stockholders would normally want the company to have a high debt-to-equity ratio.

Multiple Choice

Choose the best answer or response by placing the identifying letter in the space provided.

____ 1. Artway Corporation's net income last year was $200,000. It paid dividends of $50,000 to the owners of the company's preferred stock. There were 10,000 shares of common stock outstanding throughout the year. What was the company's earnings per share for the year? a) $20; b) $5; c) $15; d) $25.

____ 2. Carston Corporation's earnings per share is $3.50 and its market price per share is $28. There are 1 million shares of common stock outstanding. What is the company's price-earnings ratio? a) 43.75; b) 4.375; c) 80.0; d) 8.0.

____ 3. Refer to the data for Carston Corporation in question 2 above. Assume in addition that the company pays an annual dividend of $2.17 per share. What is the company's dividend payout ratio? a) 62%; b) 7.75%; c) 217%; d) 8.9%.

____ 4. Refer again to the data for Carston Corporation in questions 2 and 3 above. What is the company's dividend yield ratio? a) 62%; b) 7.75%; c) 217%; d) 8.9%.

____ 5. Darsden Corporation's net income last year was $800,000; its average assets were $4,000,000; its interest expense was $200,000; and its tax rate was 30%. What was the company's return on total assets? a) 23.5%; b) 25%; c) 16.5%; d) 30%.

____ 6. Kristal Corporation's net income last year was $600,000. The company paid preferred dividends of $200,000 to the owners of its preferred stock. The average common stockholders' equity was $5,000,000. What was the company's return on common stockholders' equity? a) 12%; b) 4%; c) 10%; d) 8%.

____ 7. Harrison Corporation's common stockholders' equity is $24 million. There are 6 million shares of common stock and 2 million shares of preferred stock outstanding. What is the company's book value per share? a) $3.00; b) $4.00; c) $6.00; d) $2.40.

____ 8. J.J. Corporation's current assets are $6 million and its current liabilities are $2 million. What is the company's working capital? a) $6 million; b) $2 million; c) $4 million; d) $8 million.

____ 9. Refer to the data for J.J. Corporation in question 8 above. What is the company's current ratio? a) 3.0 to 1; b) 2.0 to 1; c) 0.33 to 1; d) 0.50 to 1.

____ 10. Refer to the data for J.J. Corporation in question 8 above. Assume in addition that the company has $1 million in cash and marketable securities and $1.2 million in current receivables. What is the company's acid-test ratio? a) 0.8 to 1; b) 1.0 to 1; c) 1.2 to 1; d) 1.1 to 1.

____ 11. Proctor Corporation had $25 million of credit sales last year and its average accounts receivable balance was $5 million. What was the company's average collection period? a) 73 days; b) 5 days; c) 20 days; d) 84 days.

____ 12. Larimart Corporation's cost of goods sold last year was $750,000 and its average inventory balance was $300,000. What was the company's average days to sell inventory? a) 2.5 days; b) 5 days; c) 146 days; d) 912.5 days.

____ 13. Bresser Corporation's earnings before taxes last year was $42,000 and its interest expense was $6,000. What was the company's times interest earned? a) 12.5 times; b) 1.25 times; c) 80 times; d) 8.0 times.

____ 14. Nupper Corporation's total liabilities are $320,000 and its stockholders' equity is $400,000. What is the company's debt-to-equity ratio? a) 0.2 to 1; b) 1.25 to 1; c) 0.8 to 1; d) 5 to 1.

____ 15. The acid-test ratio: a) can be expected to be less than the current ratio; b) can be expected to be greater than the current ratio; c) could be either greater or less than the current ratio; d) none of these.

Exercises

14-1.   The financial statements of Amfac, Inc., are given below for the just completed year (This Year) and for the previous year (Last Year):

Amfac, Inc.
Balance Sheet
December 31

Assets

	This Year	Last Year
Cash	$ 8,000	$ 10,000
Accounts receivable, net	36,000	34,000
Inventory	40,000	32,000
Prepaid expenses	2,000	1,000
Plant and equipment, net	214,000	173,000
Total Assets	$300,000	$250,000

Liabilities & Equities

Current liabilities	$ 40,000	$ 30,000
Long-term liabilities	60,000	40,000
Preferred stock	50,000	50,000
Common stock	30,000	30,000
Retained earnings	120,000	100,000
Total liabilities and equity	$300,000	$250,000

Amfac, Inc.
Income Statement
For the Year Ended December 31

	This Year
Sales (all on account)	$450 000
Cost of goods sold	270,000
Gross margin	180,000
Operating expenses	129,000
Net operating income	51,000
Interest expense	6,000
Net income before taxes	45,000
Income taxes (30%)	13,500
Net Income	$ 31,500

Preferred dividends were $4,000 this year.

Compute the following ratios for this year:

a.   Current ratio.

b.   Acid-test ratio.

c.   Debt-to-equity ratio.

d.   Average collection period.

e.   Inventory turnover.

f.   Times interest earned.

g.   Return on total assets.

h.   Return on common stockholders' equity.

i.   Is financial leverage positive or negative? Explain.

_____

_____

_____

_____

14-2.   Cartwright Company has reported the following data relating to sales and accounts receivable in its most recent annual report

	Year 5	Year 4	Year 3	Year 2	Year 1
Sales	$700,000	$675,000	$650,000	$575,000	$500,000
Accounts receivable	$ 72,000	$ 60,000	$ 52,000	$ 46,000	$ 40,000

Express the data above in trend percentages. Use Year 1 as the base year.

	Year 5	Year 4	Year 3	Year 2	Year 1
Sales	_____	_____	_____	_____	_____
Accounts receivable	_____	_____	_____	_____	_____

Comment on the significant information revealed by your trend percentages:

_____

_____

_____

_____

14-3. Consider the following comparative income statements of Eldredge Company, a jewelry design and manufacturing company:

Eldredge Company
Income Statements
For the Years Ended December 31

	This Year	*Last Year*
Sales	$600,000	$500,000
Cost of goods sold..........................	420,000	331,000
Gross margin	180,000	169,000
Operating expenses:		
Selling expenses	87,000	72,500
Administrative expenses...............	46,800	51,000
Total operating expenses	133,800	123,500
Net operating income	46,200	45,500
Interest expense	1,200	1,500
Net income before taxes	45,000	44,000
Income taxes...................................	13,500	13,200
Net Income	$ 31,500	$ 30,800

a. Express the income statements for both years in common-size percentages. Round percentages to one decimal point.

	This Year	*Last Year*
Sales...	_____	_____
Cost of goods sold	_____	_____
Gross margin.................................	_____	_____
Operating expenses:		
Selling expenses	_____	_____
Administrative expenses	_____	_____
Total operating expenses	_____	_____
Net operating income......................	_____	_____
Interest expense	_____	_____
Net income before taxes	_____	_____
Income taxes	_____	_____
Net Income	_____	_____

b. Comment briefly on the changes between the two years.

_____

_____

_____

_____

Answers to Questions and Exercises

True or False

1. T   This is true by definition.

2. F   A common-size statement shows items in percentage form. Each item is stated as a percentage of some total of which that item is a part.

3. F   The current ratio is current assets *divided* by current liabilities.

4. F   Trend percentages would be an example of horizontal analysis.

5. T   This point is discussed in connection with question 2 above.

6. T   The net income available to the common shareholders is the amount that remains after paying preferred dividends.

7. F   The opposite is true. If the price-earnings ratio goes up, then the stock is selling for a higher market price per dollar of earnings.

8. F   Dividing the market price of a share of stock by the earnings per share gives the price-earnings ratio.

9. T   Book value per share is the balance sheet carrying value of completed transactions—it tells little about the future.

10. T   Inventories are excluded because they may be difficult to quickly convert to cash.

11. F   When computing the total return on assets, the after-tax interest expense is *added back* to net income to remove its effect.

12. F   Inventory turnover is computed by dividing cost of goods sold by average inventory.

13. T   If a company's return on total assets is higher than its cost of borrowing, then financial leverage is positive. Common stockholders would want the company to use this positive financial leverage to their advantage by having a high amount of debt in the company.

Multiple Choice

1. c   The computations are:

$$\frac{\text{Earnings}}{\text{per share}} = \frac{\text{Net income-Preferred dividends}}{\text{Average number of common shares outstanding}}$$

$$\frac{\$200,000-\$50,000}{10,000 \text{ shares}} = \$15 \text{ per share}$$

2. d   The computations are:

$$\text{Price-earnings ratio} = \frac{\text{Market price per share}}{\text{Earnings per share}}$$

$$\frac{\$28.00}{\$3.50} = 8.0$$

3. a   The computations are:

$$\text{Dividend payout ratio} = \frac{\text{Dividends per share}}{\text{Earnings per share}}$$

$$\frac{\$2.17}{\$3.50} = 62.0\%$$

4. b   The computations are:

$$\text{Dividend yield ratio} = \frac{\text{Dividends per share}}{\text{Market price per share}}$$

$$\frac{\$2.17}{\$28.00} = 7.75\%$$

5. a   The computations are:

$$\frac{\text{Return on}}{\text{total assets}} = \frac{\text{Net income} + \left[\begin{array}{c}\text{Interest expense} \times \\ (1\text{-Tax rate})\end{array}\right]}{\text{Average total assets}}$$

$$\frac{\$800,000 + \left[\begin{array}{c}\$200,000 \times \\ (1\text{-}0.30)\end{array}\right]}{\$4,000,000} = 23.5\%$$

6. d   The computations are:

$$\text{Return on common stockholers' equity} = \frac{\text{Net income} - \text{Preferred dividends}}{\text{Average common stockholders' equity}}$$

$$= \frac{\$600,000 - \$200,000}{\$5,000,000} = 8\%$$

7. b   The computations are:

$$\text{Book value per share} = \frac{\text{Common stockholders' equity}}{\text{Number of common shares outstanding}}$$

$$= \frac{\$24,000,000}{6,000,000 \text{ shares}} = \$4.00 \text{ per share}$$

8. c   The computations are:

$$\text{Working capital} = \frac{\text{Current}}{\text{assets}} - \frac{\text{Current}}{\text{liabilities}}$$

$$= \$6,000 - \$2,000 = \$4,000,000$$

9. a   The computations are:

$$\text{Current ratio} = \frac{\text{Current assets}}{\text{Current liabilities}}$$

$$= \frac{\$6,000,000}{\$2,000,000} = 3.0$$

10. d   The computations are:

$$\text{Acid-test ratio} = \frac{\text{Cash} + \text{Marketable securities} + \text{Current receivables}}{\text{Current liabilities}}$$

$$= \frac{\$1,000,000 + \$1,200,000}{\$2,000,000} = 1.1$$

11. a   The computations are:

$$\text{Accounts receivable turnover} = \frac{\text{Sales on account}}{\text{Average accounts receivable balance}}$$

$$= \frac{\$25,000,000}{\$5,000,000} = 5.0$$

$$\text{Average collection period} = \frac{365 \text{ days}}{\text{Accounts receivable turnover}}$$

$$= \frac{365 \text{ days}}{5.0} = 73 \text{ days}$$

12. c   The computations are:

$$\text{Inventory turnover} = \frac{\text{Cost of goods sold}}{\text{Average inventory balance}}$$

$$= \frac{\$750,000}{\$300,000} = 2.5$$

$$\text{Average sale period} = \frac{365 \text{ days}}{\text{Inventory turnover}}$$

$$= \frac{365 \text{ days}}{2.5} = 146 \text{ days}$$

13. d   The computations are:

$$\text{Times interest earned} = \frac{\text{Earnings before interest expense and income taxes}}{\text{Interest expense}}$$

$$= \frac{\$42,000 + \$6,000}{\$6,000} = 8.0$$

14. c   The computations are:

$$\text{Debt-to-equity ratio} = \frac{\text{Total liabilities}}{\text{Stockholders' equity}}$$

$$= \frac{\$320,000}{\$400,000} = 0.8$$

15. a   The acid-test ratio will always be less than the current ratio because it contains fewer assets in the numerator but the same amount of liabilities in the denominator.

Exercises

14-1.

a. $\text{Current ratio} = \dfrac{\text{Current assets}}{\text{Current liabilities}} = \dfrac{\$8,000+\$36,000+\$40,000+\$2,000}{\$40,000} = 2.15$

b. $\dfrac{\text{Acid-test}}{\text{ratio}} = \dfrac{\substack{\text{Cash + Marketable securities} \\ \text{+ Current receivables}}}{\text{Current liabilities}} = \dfrac{\$8,000+\$36,000}{\$40,000} = 1.10$

c. $\dfrac{\text{Debt-to-equity}}{\text{ratio}} = \dfrac{\text{Total liabilities}}{\text{Stockholders' equity}} = \dfrac{\$40,000+\$60,000}{\$50,000+\$30,000+\$120,000} = 0.50$

d. $\dfrac{\text{Accounts receivable}}{\text{turnover}} = \dfrac{\text{Sales on account}}{\substack{\text{Average accounts} \\ \text{receivable balance}}} = \dfrac{\$450,000}{(\$36,000+\$34,000)/2} = 12.9 \text{ (rounded)}$

$\dfrac{\text{Average collection}}{\text{period}} = \dfrac{365 \text{ days}}{\text{Accounts receivable turnover}} = \dfrac{365 \text{ days}}{12.9} = 28 \text{ days (rounded)}$

e. $\dfrac{\text{Inventory}}{\text{turnover}} = \dfrac{\text{Cost of goods sold}}{\text{Average inventory balance}} = \dfrac{\$270,000}{(\$40,000+\$32,000)/2} = 7.5$

f. $\dfrac{\text{Times interest}}{\text{earned}} = \dfrac{\substack{\text{Earnings before interest expense} \\ \text{and income taxes}}}{\text{Interest expense}} = \dfrac{\$51,000}{\$6,000} = 8.5$

g. $\dfrac{\text{Return on}}{\text{total assets}} = \dfrac{\text{Net income} + \left[\substack{\text{Interest expense} \times \\ (1\text{-Tax rate})}\right]}{\text{Average total assets}} = \dfrac{\$31,500 + \left[\substack{\$6,000 \times \\ (1\text{-}0.30)}\right]}{(\$300,000+\$250,000)/2} = 13.0\% \text{ (rounded)}$

h.

	End of Year	*Beginning of Year*
Total stockholders' equity	$200,000	$180,000
Less preferred stock...................................	50,000	50,000
Common stockholders' equity	$150,000	$130,000

$\dfrac{\text{Return on common}}{\text{stockholers' equity}} = \dfrac{\substack{\text{Net income} - \\ \text{Preferred dividends}}}{\substack{\text{Average common} \\ \text{stockholders' equity}}} = \dfrac{\$31,500 - \$4,000}{(\$150,000+\$130,000)/2} = 19.6\% \text{ (rounded)}$

i. Financial leverage is positive, since the return on the common stockholders' equity is greater than the return on total assets.

14-2.

	Year 5	Year 4	Year 3	Year 2	Year 1
Sales	140%	135%	130%	115%	100%
Accounts receivable	180%	150%	130%	115%	100%

Sales grew by about 15% per year through Year 3, and then dropped off to about a 5% growth rate for the next two years. The accounts receivable grew at about a 15% rate through Year 3, but then rather than dropping off to about a 5% rate, the accounts receivable grew at an even faster rate through Year 5. This suggests that the company may be granting credit too liberally and is having difficulty collecting.

14-3.

a.

Eldredge Company
Common-Size Comparative Income Statements
For the Years Ended December 31

	This Year	Last Year
Sales..	100.0	100.0
Cost of goods sold	70.0	66.2
Gross margin	30.0	33.8
Operating expenses:		
Selling expenses	14.5	14.5
Administrative expenses....................	7.8	10.2
Total operating expenses	22.3	24.7
Net operating income............................	7.7	9.1
Interest expense	0.2	0.3
Net income before taxes	7.5	8.8
Income taxes..	2.2	2.6
Net Income	5.3	6.2

b.   Cost of goods sold and administrative expenses were the two primary areas affecting the percentage decrease in net income. Cost of goods sold increased from 66.2% of sales in to 70.0% of sales—an increase of 3.8%. On the other hand, administrative expenses dropped from 10.2% of sales to only 7.8% of sales—a decrease of 2.4%. The net effect was a decrease in net income as a percentage of sales, which fell from 6.2% of sales to only 5.3% of sales. The increase in the cost of goods sold as a percentage of sales is puzzling since sales increased. Ordinarily, cost of goods sold as a percentage of sales should decrease as sales increase because fixed production costs are spread across more units.